Inhalt

Allgemeiner Teil 2

Topicbegleitender Teil

Topic 1: Global challenges
Didaktisches Inhaltsverzeichnis 6
Unterrichtsverlauf 8

Topic 2: Think globally, eat locally?
Didaktisches Inhaltsverzeichnis 29
Unterrichtsverlauf 30

Topic 3: Saving the planet
Didaktisches Inhaltsverzeichnis 40
Unterrichtsverlauf 42

Topic 4: International peacekeeping
Didaktisches Inhaltsverzeichnis 58
Unterrichtsverlauf 60

Anhang

1 Sequenzplaner – Differenzierungshinweise GK/LK 91

2 Kopiervorlagen 93

3 Lösungen zu den Kopiervorlagen 102

4 Klausurvorschläge 103

5 Erwartungshorizont zu den Klausurvorschlägen 111

6 Erwartungshorizont zu den *Revision files* 118

AT | Allgemeiner Teil

Allgemeiner Teil

Reihenkonzept Das Heft *Globalisation* ist ein Themenheft aus der Reihe „Abi Workshop Englisch". Diese Reihe bietet eine Sammlung von Themen- und Methodenheften, die speziell auf die Erfordernisse der G8-Oberstufe und der zentralen Abiturprüfung ausgerichtet sind und ohne den Einsatz eines Oberstufen-Lehrwerks eine gründliche Vorbereitung des Abiturs gewährleisten. Während die

Methodenhefte Methodenhefte konsequent methoden- und kompetenzorientiert sind, bieten die Themenhefte einen landeskundlich-interkulturell ausgerichteten Überblick über ein relevantes Abiturthema.

Themenhefte Im Themenheft *Globalisation* sind die konzeptionellen Neuerungen der Reihe „Abi Workshop Englisch" auf folgende Weise realisiert:

Dokumenten CD-ROM

CD-ROM Auf der Dokumenten CD-ROM sind die Hörtexte, die Filmsequenzen und die *Vocabulary sheets* enthalten. Dadurch, dass die CD-ROM den Schülern und Schülerinnen (künftig: S) und Lehrern und Lehrerinnen (künftig: L) gleichermaßen zur Verfügung steht, können wichtige Lernbereiche deutlich intensiver behandelt werden als bisher. Für die S besteht die Möglichkeit zur Nachbereitung der Lernbereiche Hörverstehen bzw. Hör-/Sehverstehen sowie zu einer systematischen selbstständigen Wortschatzarbeit in der Oberstufe. Für die L bietet sich die Gelegenheit, diese Lernbereiche in die Unterrichtsvorbereitung durch die S einzubeziehen und sie zusätzlich auch für Hausaufgaben zu nutzen. Das Schülerheft *Globalisation* enthält dementsprechend ausführliche Aufgabenstellungen.

Hör-/ Sehverstehen Für die weitere Schulung des Hör-/Sehverstehens stehen drei Videoclips zur Verfügung, die mit einem ausführlichen Aufgabenapparat im Schülerheft versehen sind. Die Benutzung der Filmausschnitte im Klassenzimmer ist ausdrücklich gestattet. Darüber hinaus enthält das Schülerheft *Globalisation* zahlreiche Aufgaben und Online-Links, sodass Hör-/Sehverstehen ohne die üblichen Probleme bei der Materialbeschaffung möglich ist. Insgesamt wird die Behandlung dieses Lernbereichs erheblich ausgeweitet und intensiviert.

Vokabelkonzept Das Themenheft *Globalisation* ermöglicht den S eine systematische und erfolgsorientierte Wortschatzarbeit in der Oberstufe, die eine optimale Vorbereitung auf das Abitur gewährleistet. Dazu wurde die Vokabelarbeit folgendermaßen organisiert:

Wortschatz im Themenheft

Topics Der in den *Topics* angegebene Wortschatz dient ausschließlich dem Verständnis der Texte bzw. als Hilfe für die Bewältigung von Aufgaben. Der im Textteil angegebene Wortschatz ist **nicht identisch** mit dem Lernvokabular auf der CD-ROM. Die Wörter sind in unterschiedlicher Weise aufbereitet:

Annotations • Die *Annotations* dienen zur Erklärung nicht erschließbarer, für das Textverständnis zentraler Wörter und Begriffe. Sie stehen in der Randspalte und enthalten bei Bedarf auch die phonetische Umschrift.

Useful phrases • Unter dem Titel *Useful phrases* finden die S eine Zusammenstellung von Wörtern und Wendungen – bekannten und neuen – zur Bewältigung einer Diskussions- oder Kommentierungsaufgabe. Die roten Kästchen stehen unmittelbar bei der Aufgabe.

Word bank • Unter dem Titel *Word bank* erhalten die S eine Zusammenstellung von auf das Thema bezogenen Wörtern – bekannten und neuen – zur thematischen Bewältigung der Aufgaben. Die roten Kästchen mit diesen Wörtern stehen in der Regel auf den Auftaktseiten (*to help students get started*).

Allgemeiner Teil | **AT**

Vocabulary sheets auf der CD-ROM

CD-ROM Die Organisation des Wortschatzes geschieht mit Hilfe der *Vocabulary sheets* auf der CD-ROM. Das Schülerheft bzw. Themenheft enthält lediglich zwei Seiten als Muster mit Erläuterungen (Seite 57/58). Das Themenheft bietet eine dreispaltige Vorlage zur Gestaltung der *Vocabulary sheets* an:

Gestaltung
- Die linke Spalte ist für die zu erlernende Vokabel bestimmt (Einzelwort oder Wendung).
- Die mittlere Spalte kann Antonyme, Synonyme, Bezüge zur Wortfamilie usw. enthalten. Bei Einzelwörtern in der linken Spalte bietet sie vor allem wichtige Kollokationen.
- Die rechte Spalte ist für die deutsche Übersetzung der Lernvokabel und wichtiger Kollokationen vorgesehen.

Editierbar Die *Vocabulary sheets* werden für die S in einer Version mit Lücken angeboten. In der Regel ist nur die linke Spalte gefüllt und damit der zu lernende Wortschatz definiert. Es ist die Aufgabe der S, die leeren Spalten im Rahmen der Textarbeit zu füllen. Auf diese Weise erarbeiten sie sich den chronologischen Wortschatz weitgehend selbstständig. Der Inhalt der mittleren und rechten Spalte wird nur punktuell vorgegeben, um Variationsmöglichkeiten zu eröffnen und den S immer wieder Hinweise auf Vernetzungstechniken für die Wortschatzarbeit zu geben. Durch die Editierbarkeit der Word-Dokumente haben die S die Gelegenheit, jederzeit nach Wunsch weiteres Vokabular hinzuzufügen.

Online-Link Für L steht das komplett ausgefüllte Vokabular zusätzlich online bei www.klett.de zur
601012-0001 Verfügung. Der Online-Link des Lehrerheftes lautet: 601012-0001. Auf diese Weise besteht die Möglichkeit, jederzeit Vokabeltests schreiben zu lassen und diese auf komfortable Weise korrigieren zu können.

Organisation der Wortschatzarbeit

Chronologisch Aus der Reihenfolge der Vokabeln in den Texten ergibt sich ein chronologischer textbezogener Aufbau des Lernwortschatzes. Insgesamt können die S auf diese Weise einen Lernwortschatz von ca. 400–500 Wörtern pro Themenheft aufbauen. Die CD-ROM bietet zusätzlich *Vocabulary sheets* zu bestimmten Themengebieten an. In diesen Listen sind die wichtigsten Vokabeln pro Themengebiet enthalten. Ein Großteil dieser Vokabeln ergibt sich aus den Texten und ist bereits im chronologischen Wortschatz zu finden. Wichtiger, noch fehlender Wortschatz wird
Thematisch ergänzt, sodass die S am Ende thematisch gruppierte Lernwortlisten vorliegen haben, die es ihnen ermöglichen, sich optimal auf die mündliche oder schriftliche Textproduktion zu einem bestimmten Thema vorzubereiten. Der Inhalt der Wortlisten zu bestimmten Texten oder Themen kann von L als verbindlich erklärt und ggf. in Vokabeltests überprüft werden. L und S können somit unabhängig voneinander entscheiden, ob sie nur mit den chronologischen oder auch mit den thematischen Wortlisten arbeiten möchten.

Topics im Themenheft

Topics Das Themenheft *Globalisation* enthält vier *Topics:*
Topic 1: *Global challenges*
Topic 2: *Think globally, eat locally?*
Topic 3: *Saving the planet*
Topic 4: *International peacekeeping*

Tasks Die *Topics* bieten ein vielseitiges und abwechslungsreiches Übungsangebot mit dem Ziel, die S zu einer textsortengerechten Produktion von gesprochener und geschriebener Sprache zu befähigen. Dabei stehen die Anforderungen der Abiturprüfung selbst und die Bewältigung der verschiedenen Lern- und Arbeitsbereiche der Oberstufe im Mittelpunkt. Grundsätzlich orientiert sich das Übungsangebot an den Anforderungsbereichen *Comprehension, Analysis*
Operatoren und *Evaluation* sowie an der Erarbeitung der jeweiligen Operatoren. Darüber hinaus ermöglicht die Übungsfolge in dem Themenheft *Globalisation* einen lebendigen und motivierenden Unterricht. Neben den textanalytischen Fragestellungen spielen auch Aufgaben zu den
Kompetenzen Kompetenzen eine wichtige Rolle. Dies sind u. a. *Discussing, Debating,* Recherche (auch über

3

	Online-Links), Präsentation, Projekte, *Creative writing*, Wortschatzaufbau, *Mediation*, Hörver-stehen, Hör-/Sehverstehen, Ergebnissicherung. Die Übungen sind für die unterschiedlichsten
Sozialformen	Sozialformen konzipiert. Häufig wird Gruppen- oder Partnerarbeit empfohlen. Durch die sinnvolle Kombination der verschiedenen Aufgaben entsteht so ein anregendes Übungsan-gebot, das die zielgerichtete Vorbereitung auf die Abiturprüfung gewährleistet, gleichzeitig aber die immer wiederkehrende Umwälzung durch nur wenige gleichförmige Übungsformate verhindert. Das Übungsangebot im Themenheft *Globalisation* orientiert sich damit auch an der Verwendung der englischen Sprache über das Abitur hinaus.

Servicematerial im Anhang

Projects
Das Themenheft *Globalisation* enthält im Anhang (Seite 50–56) drei Projektvorschläge:
Project 1: Three advertising campaigns targeting young people
Project 2: Conducting a talk show on globalisation
Project 3: Conducting a Security Council debate on a global crisis
Die *Projects* sind in mehrere *Steps* untergliedert und die S erhalten zusätzlich Strategien zur Umsetzung:
- *How to use a strategy to advertise a product*
- *How to make a radio commercial*
- *How to make a printed advertisement*
- *Taking part in a discussion – 24 strategies with useful phrases*
- *How to chair a discussion*

Worksheets
Nach den *Projects* finden die S im Themenheft Informationen zur Konzeption der Wortschatz-arbeit (Seite 57/58). Hier wird die Organisation der *Vocabulary sheets* erläutert und die S finden Muster einer textbezogenen chronologischen und einer thematischen Wortschatzseite mit Hinweisen zur Verwendung:
- *How to work with the text-based vocabulary files*
- *How to work with the thematic vocabulary files*

Revision files
Zu jedem der vier *Topics* wird eine methodisch jeweils modifizierte *Revision file* angeboten (Seite 59–62), in die die S die wichtigsten Daten und Informationen eintragen können. Die *Revision files* sind ein Instrument zur Ergebnissicherung und zur Wiederholung. Sie können gezielt zur Klausur- oder Prüfungsvorbereitung eingesetzt werden. Ein Erwartungshorizont befindet sich hier im Lehrerheft im Anhang (Seite 118–120).

Methodenhefte

Methodenhefte
Das Themenheft *Globalisation* kann ideal ergänzt werden durch eine Auswahl aus den ebenfalls im „Abi Workshop Englisch" zur Verfügung stehenden Methodenheften. Je nach den Notwendigkeiten der Lerngruppe können gezielt Defizite aufgearbeitet oder besondere Schwerpunkte gesetzt werden. Auch die individuelle Förderung von S ist möglich. Alle Methodenhefte sind konsequent auf die Anforderungen der Oberstufe und des Abiturs ausgerichtet. Sie sind sowohl für den Klassenunterricht als auch für das Selbststudium geeignet. Die jeweils beiliegende CD-ROM enthält alle Lösungen und Erwartungshorizonte.

Lehrerheft

Lehrerheft
Das Lehrerheft setzt sich zum Ziel, einen wirksamen Beitrag zu einer effektiven und zeit-sparenden Unterrichtsvorbereitung und -durchführung zu leisten. Die folgenden Elemente dienen in besonderer Weise zur Arbeitserleichterung:

Didaktisches Inhaltsverzeichnis
Eine Erstinformation über die Inhalte der *Topics* bietet ein didaktisches Inhaltsverzeichnis, das in knapper und übersichtlicher Form über ‚Textsorte/Thema', ‚Unterrichtsmethoden', *Input boxes*', ‚Kompetenzen' und ‚Textproduktion' informiert. Hier sind außerdem die Textlängen (Wortanzahl) und Erscheinungsjahre der Originaltexte verzeichnet.

Allgemeiner Teil | **AT**

Unterrichtsverlauf | Es folgen Hinweise zum Unterrichtsverlauf, einschließlich der Hintergrundinformationen, methodischen Schritte, dem Lernvokabular, aller Unterrichtsergebnisse, Querverweise, Alternativen, Hausaufgaben, Zusatzmaterialien usw. Die methodisch-didaktischen Erläuterungen werden zugunsten einer knappen, übersichtlichen Benutzerführung z.T.

Ergebnis-sicherung | stichwortartig angeboten. Besonderer Wert wurde auf die Sicherung der Unterrichtsergebnisse in Form von Lösungsvorschlägen gelegt. Bei zahlreichen Texten und Übungen gibt es ausführlichere Vorschläge, insbesondere dann, wenn die Unterrichtsergebnisse für die Klausur- und Prüfungsvorbereitung relevant sind und sich auf elementare oder für die S schwierige Lernbereiche erstrecken (z. B. bei den Form-Inhalt-Beziehungen). Die S erhalten so die Chance, ihr Wissen und ihre Methodenkompetenz systematisch aufzubauen, das Gelernte zu vernetzen und – vor allem – noch einmal nachzuschauen, wenn etwas vergessen wurde.

Servicematerial im Anhang

Sequenzplaner | Im Anhang des Lehrerhefts befinden sich weitere nützliche Materialien für die Unterrichts-planung. Den Auftakt bildet ein Sequenzplaner (Seite 91/92), der in knapper und übersichtlicher Form Aufschluss über die Kernsequenzen und die Vertiefungsmaterialien gibt. Damit wird die Zuordnung der Texte für Grund- und Leistungskurse auf einen Blick deutlich.

Kopiervorlagen | Es folgen zu jedem der vier *Topics* zwei weiterführende Arbeitsblätter als Kopiervorlagen (Seite 93–101). Die Kopiervorlagen (KVs) vertiefen die behandelten Themen und dienen entweder zur Festigung des Lernwortschatzes oder zur inhaltlichen Erweiterung der Themenbereiche. Den Abschluss bildet ein *card game* (KV 8/8a, Seite 100/101) zur Anwendung der *24 discussion strategies* aus dem Anhang des Themenhefts (Seite 55).

Lösungen | Die Lösungen stehen auf Seite 102 ebenfalls als Kopiervorlage zur Verfügung. Sie können den S nach der Bearbeitung der Wortschatz-KVs 3 und 7 zur Selbstkontrolle ausgehändigt werden.

Klausur-vorschläge | Neben den Kopiervorlagen befindet sich im Anhang zu jedem *Topic* ein Klausurvorschlag (Seite 103–110). Bei *Topic* 1 und 4 handelt es sich um eine Rede, bei *Topic* 2 und 3 um einen Nachrichtenartikel aus dem Internet. Der notwendige Wortschatz wird unter dem Text als *Annotations* angeboten, darauf folgt eine Auswahl an abwechslungsreichen *Tasks*.

Erwartungs-horizont | Zu den vier Klausurvorschlägen gibt es für die Hand der L einen Erwartungshorizont (Seite 111–117). Neben den Lösungsvorschlägen zu den *Tasks* befinden sich hier die nötigen Textinforma-tionen und Quellenangaben.

Revision files | Den Abschluss des Serviceteil im Lehrerbuch bildet der Erwartungshorizont zu den *Revision files* (Seite 118–120).

Weitere Quellen

Books
- Liza Featherstone, *United Students Against Sweatshops*, Verso Publishers, 2002 (120 pages, ISBN 1859843026)
- Naomi Klein, *No Logo*, Picador, 2000, (490 pages, paperback, ISBN 0-312-27192-1)
- Felipe Fernandez-Armesto, *Millennium: A History of the Last Thousand Years*, (Simon and Schuster, 1996.
- Richard Falk, *Predatory Globalisation – A Critique*, Polity Press, 1999.
- Thomas L. Friedman, *The Lexus and the Olive Tree*, Doubleday and Company, 2000.
- Samuel Huntington, *The Clash of Civilisations and the Re-Making of World Order*, Simon and Schuster, 1997.

Website | *For further texts on globalisation see:* http://yaleglobal.yale.edu/globalization/.

Debate | *Globalisation debate between English-speaking pupils live on the Internet:* http://www.abc.net.au/global/history/history_debate.htm.

1   Global challenges   Didaktisches Inhaltsverzeichnis

Topic 1: Global challenges

pp. 4–17

Didaktisches Inhaltsverzeichnis

Bearbeitungszeitraum: 16–18 Unterrichtsstunden

Textsorte/Thema	Unterrichts-methoden	*Input boxes*	Kompetenzen	Textproduktion
Global challenges			SB, Seite 4/5; LB, Seite 8/9	
Combination of visuals/Effects of globalisation	*Classroom project* Kursgespräch Partnerarbeit	*Word bank* *Tip: What's right?*	Orientierungswissen Sehverstehen Recherchieren Gespräche führen Bildbeschreibung/-analyse	*Describing and assessing pictures Making a mind-map Writing a definition*
[1 ◉] Globalization blues, 2002 (111 words)			SB, Seite 5; LB, Seite 10	
American song/ Protest song		*Fact file: Protest song*	Hörverstehen Leseverstehen Form-Inhalt-Beziehungen erkennen Recherchieren	*Working with a song Presenting a song*
[2 ◉] The three eras of globalization, 2006 (743 words)			SB, Seite 6/7; LB, Seite 11–14	
American book excerpt (non-fiction)/History of globalisation	Gruppenarbeit Online-Link 1	*Fact files: Christopher Columbus/The Dutch East India Company VIP file: Thomas L. Friedman Useful phrases: Individual opportunities*	Recherchieren Hörverstehen Leseverstehen Gespräche führen Bildbeschreibung/-analyse	*Describing and assessing pictures Making a mind-map Making a timeline, poster or fact file Creative writing*
Spot on facts, 2008 (423 words)			SB, Seite 8; LB, Seite 15/16	
Definition of globalisation, basic global trends and hopes and fears	Zusatzmaterial: Kopiervorlage 1, Kopiervorlage 2	*Fact file on globalisation*	Orientierungswissen Leseverstehen	
[1 🎞] The corporation, 2004 (840 words)			SB, Seite 9; LB, Seite 16–18	
Canadian documentary film/ Ruthless fight of corporations for money and power	*Video transcript* (CD-ROM) Partnerarbeit Online-Link 2	*Useful phrases: Talking about characteristics*	Hörverstehen Sehverstehen Gespräche führen	*Looking up definitions Talking about characteristics Finding idioms*
[3 ◉] Sourcing global talent in software, 2007 (414 words)			SB, Seite 10/11; LB, Seite 18–20	
American news-paper interview/ (Out)sourcing of work		*Fact file: Sourcing Useful phrases: Writing a suggestion*	Hörverstehen Leseverstehen Recherchieren Gespräche führen	*Writing a summary/ an outline Writing a formal letter*
Cartooning outsourcing			SB, Seite 11; LB, Seite 20	
Cartoons/(Out) sourcing of work			Gespräche führen Argumentieren	*Talking about a cartoon*

Global challenges Didaktisches Inhaltsverzeichnis **1**

Textsorte/Thema	Unterrichts-methoden	*Input boxes*	Kompetenzen	Textproduktion
Moving goods around the globe, 2006 (768 words)			SB, Seite 12/13; LB, Seite 20–22	
British magazine article/Globalisa-tion and the freight business		*Tip: -isation* *Useful phrases:* *Presenting a statement*	Leseverstehen	*Working with a diagram* *Presenting a statement* *Making a comment*
Frischer Wind für Frachter, 2007 (347 words)			SB, Seite 14; LB, Seite 22/23	
German magazine article/ Equipping freighters with kites to reduce CO2 emissions	Partnerarbeit Online-Link 3		Mediation Leseverstehen	*Conducting an interview*
[4 ◎] My global mind, 2004 (194 words)			SB, Seite 15; LB, Seite 23–25	
American song/ Criticism on globalisation and its negative impact on the individual		*Fact file: Poverty* *Useful phrases:* *Commenting on an idea*	Hörverstehen Leseverstehen	*Working with a song* *Writing a definition* *Making a comment*
Is American culture 'American'?, 2006 (693 words)			SB, Seite 16/17; LB, Seite 25–28	
American scholarly article/Influence of American culture in the world	Partnerarbeit Gruppenarbeit Zusatzmaterial: Klausur-vorschlag 1	*Useful phrases:* *Analysing a text*	Gespräche führen Argumentieren Leseverstehen	*Giving a speech* *Giving a definition* *Making a comment*

7

1 Global challenges · Lead-in: Global challenges

Unterrichtsverlauf

Photos

Lead-in: Global challenges · pp. 4/5

HINTERGRUNDINFO

Sweatshops *can be found all over the world. Their characteristics are long working hours, low wages and bad working conditions. The aim of those factories, which came into existence in the industrialisation era, is the cheapest production possible of bulk goods.*

DHL *is an acronym for the company's three founders' surnames: Dalsey, Hillblom and Lynn. It is a* Deutsche Post *company offering international shipping of documents and freight as well as contract logistics. The business was founded in 1969 and started by providing air express delivery in the US. In 2002 Deutsche Post, which had already gained the major ownership the year before, purchased DHL. In 2005 the company employed more than 11,000 people in 135 countries.*

Protest songs *usually deal with issues of society or global conflicts. In the middle of the 18th century the*

first political songs were written as a response to social injustice. Popular melodies were often used for the new lyrics. An early and very famous kind of protest song is the Negro spiritual from the 19th century. Some of the most famous protest songs come from the US. Among them are "We Shall Overcome", Bob Dylan's "Blowin' in the Wind" and Marvin Gaye's "What's going on?".

Globalisation, *example for definition (refers to task 4; see also definition in Fact file, p. 8): Globalisation is the worldwide process of connecting industries and countries with each other in regard to their economic, technological, sociocultural and political forces. The rapid development of technology, especially the communication sector, caused an immense acceleration in the process as well as a large extension of its scope. Globalisation also affects culture, politics and other areas of society.*

Discussion
L verweist auf die *Word bank words* und stellt den S zum Einstieg einige Fragen bzw. Aufforderungen als Impulse:
What is the connection between the pictures on pp. 4/5 and globalisation?
What appears to be strange in the first picture?
Which values are presented in the 4th picture?
Describe the 5th picture in detail and discuss whether you think this woman can change anything.
Explain the caption under the photo of the polar bear.

Survey

1 Classroom project

L oder S überträgt die Tabelle in Aufgabe **a)** auf Folie und füllt sie aus. Aufgabe **b)** wird anschließend im Plenum besprochen.

Lösungsvorschlag
b) *A comparison of several objects like accessories and clothes shows that the majority of them are produced in Asian countries like Thailand or China. This could lead to the assumption that cheap products have their origin in Third World countries. It is, however, surprising that not only the cheap discounters sell products from Asian factories, but also all of the high-quality designer labels are imported from there. The difference in quality and origin between expensive and no-name clothes is therefore not obvious. One could conclude that the whole industry has become an important part of globalisation. Hardly anything is produced in Western Europe or the United States but everyone abuses the cheap workforces in Third World countries. Globalisation in industry has therefore a negative connotation as a lot of factories are outsourced into countries with less expensive working conditions and cheaper production costs. By getting into the details and realising what globalisation means to industry, one could acquire a critical point of view on globalisation. This might be surprising for many of us, as globalisation is often mentioned with positive connections.*

Global challenges **Lead-in: Global challenges** **1**

Discussion **2 How did the objects that were not made here …**

Die S überlegen, wie die Transportwege und Arbeitsbedingungen aussehen, die mit der Herstellung und dem Transport der Gegenstände/Artikel zusammenhängen.

Lösungsvorschlag *It is generally agreed that globalisation in industry means minimising costs by using foreign workforces or even moving whole factories to Third World countries. Therefore, one could assume that working conditions in these factories do not even approximately meet the standards in Western Europe or the United States. Factories and companies try to save money in production and transport. Workers in Third World countries might probably suffer from bad working conditions with long working hours, only few breaks and a wage that is not comparable to European standards. Attempts are made to keep transport costs down by not adhering to international safety regulations. Although we pay less for the items produced in Asian countries we have to ask ourselves whether we can agree to the process of abusing Third World workers through bad working conditions. All the products collected in the classroom came from Asian countries and went through the hands of those workers. Everyone should keep that in mind when talking about globalisation.*

Discussion **3 Why were none of these objects produced in Germany?**

Als Beispiel kann L bei Aufgabe **a)** auf Nokia hinweisen: Nokia Handys wurden bis 2008 in Bochum produziert. Die Produktion wurde wegen geringerer Lohnkosten von Deutschland nach Rumänien verlagert. Auch bei den anderen Produkten dürften die Lohnkosten sowie die Notwendigkeit der Präsenz vor Ort die ausschlaggebenden Gründe für die Produktions-verlagerung gewesen sein. L erinnert bei Aufgabe **b)** an die Tradition *Made in Germany*, die nach dem 2. Weltkrieg begründet wurde und lange Zeit als Zeichen für Qualität galt.

Lösungsvorschlag *a)/b)* *Hardly any of the products are produced in Western Europe or even in Germany any longer. The reasons for this are not difficult to figure out: In Germany working conditions and working hours are restricted by many laws. Companies have to pay money for various insurance items for their workforces and the employees are only allowed to work up to eight hours. In Third World countries they can save all these costs and produce much more cheaply. Factories are built in countries with cheaper working conditions and wages in these countries are far below the average income of a European worker. Modern industry is founded on making a profit. The companies' calculations are easy: the more money a company can save during the production process the higher is their profit. Reflecting on this we understand why only few things are still produced in Germany. After World War II the label "Made in Germany" was a synonym for quality. From the 1960s to the 1980s many things were produced in Germany. The situation changed rapidly in the 90s of the last century with the breakdown of communism and the outsourcing of factories to Third World countries.*

Discussion **4 [⚇] With a partner, make a mind-map …**

Die *mind-map* soll während der Bearbeitung von *Topic* 1 sukzessive ergänzt werden, deshalb planen die S eine komplette A4-Seite ein. Zum Vergleich mit der S-Definition führt L die folgende wissenschaftliche Definition ein. Die S konkretisieren die abstrakte Begrifflichkeit durch Beispiele: *"Globalisation refers to a multidimensional set of social processes that create, multiply, stretch, and intensify worldwide social interdependencies and exchanges while at the same time fostering in people a growing awareness of deepening connections between the local and the distant."* (Manfred B. Steger, in: *Globalisation. A Very Short Introduction*, Oxford University Press, 2003, p. 13.)

Lösungsvorschlag *Easy definition: exchange of goods, services and ideas across borders.*

9

1 Global challenges — Globalization blues

Protest song **[1◉] Globalization blues** — p. 5

HINTERGRUNDINFO

Ray Korona writes and performs political, environmental and labour folk and folk rock and also love songs, touring nationally both solo and with the Ray Korona Band. Despite Ray's outspoken lyrics, his music has found its way onto NPR, Pacifica & hundreds of college & community radio stations. Ray has co-written, recorded and performed music with Pete Seeger, shared the stage with speakers such as Amy Goodman, Noam Chomsky, Greg Palast and singers such as Tom Paxton, Patti Smith, and Richie Havens. Ray's songs have been published in many languages by the UN's International Labor Office; he was quoted in a cover story in "New York Magazine", won the Mobilization for Survival's peace song contest and has performed at major international gatherings.

Lernwortschatz globalisation, to be worse off than sb/sth, sweatshop (pej), to be in debt, slave made, world trade

Materialien → CD, Track 1

Analysis **5 Make a list of the aspects of globalisation …**

[1◉] Bevor Aufgabe 5 bearbeitet wird, spielt L **Track 1** zweimal von der CD-ROM vor.

Lösungsvorschlag a) *Increase in crime, poor working conditions and low wages, loss of individuals' freedom. There is not a single positive aspect of globalisation in the song.*
b) 1. *No escape/More crime through globalisation*
2. *Working hard for nothing/Abuse of market power*
3. *Loss of independence/"Global slaves" for the world market*
4. *Fight globalisation!/Fight back now!/Don't let globalisation oppress you!*
c) • *The use of compounds (l. 5: drug-dealing, money-stealing; l. 10: people-bashing, job-smashing; l. 15: slave-made, world-trade) shows how a new world order requires new words.*
• *"They" vs. "you" leads to feelings of alienation.*
• *Clear statements (l. 3: you'll be worse off than dead) suggest that the singer is convinced of what he says.*
• *A "strong" and "violent" vocabulary (l. 3: they'll run over you; l. 10: people-bashing, job-smashing", l. 17: fight; l. 20: beat) reflects what globalisation does to people.*

Effect: *Overall, the choice of words threatens the listener and stresses that globalisation is an immediate and urgent danger to the listener. The word choice also tries to persuade the listener to act now (l. 17: fight; l. 20: beat) and to strengthen the individual (l. 20: "you" becomes "we"). The singer is still hopeful and believes that the "battle" is not lost yet.*

Evaluation **6 Presentation**

Mit Medienunterstützung halten die S eine ca. 10-minütige Präsentation über einen von ihnen gewählten Protestsong. Die S vergleichen die *Song*-Aussage mit ihrer eigenen und/oder Stegers Definition von Globalisierung und arbeiten die Unterschiede heraus *(chances and risks of globalisation)*.

Erweiterung Links zu weiteren Protestsongs:
- *Songs With a Global Conscience:*
  www.rethinkingschools.org/publication/rg/RGResource01.shtml
- *Videos With a Global Conscience:*
  www.rethinkingschools.org/publication/rg/RGResource02.shtml
- *Song lyrics, for activists and protests:* www.ocap.ca/lyrics.html
  (This is a listing of song lyrics of inspiration, for protest and for activist on topics including poverty, environmentalism, racism, police brutality, greed and even landlords!)
- *Greatest Eighties Protest Songs:* www.inthe80s.com/protest.shtml

Global challenges The three eras of globalization **1**

Book excerpt **[2◉] The three eras of globalization** pp. 6/7

HINTERGRUNDINFO

Thomas L. Friedman *started his career as a financial reporter for the New York Times; later: chief diplomatic, chief White House and international economic correspondent. He runs a column dealing with foreign affairs that appears twice a week and has won the Pulitzer Prize three times for international reporting and commentary. Friedman is also author of several books, e.g. "The Lexus and the Olive Tree" (2000, translated into 20 languages), "The World is Flat. A Brief History of the 21st Century" (2005, a bestseller, translated into 25 languages). Born in Minneapolis in 1953, he took his degree in Mediterranean studies at Brandeis University and later received his master's degree in modern Middle East studies at Oxford. Friedman is married and lives with his wife and two children in Maryland.*

Christopher Columbus *(c. 1451–1506) was born and grew up in Genua. As a young man he became a sailor. Landing in Portugal after one of his trips, he lived there for several years. Columbus wanted to find a new trade route to the Indias, an idea that was popular among explorers and tradesmen at the time. After asking the Spanish King for his financial*

support, he left Europe and landed on an island on the Bahamas, thus becoming known as the first European to "discover" America.

Marco Polo *(1254–1324) was a Venetian merchant and author whose account of his travels and experiences in China offered Europeans a firsthand view of Asia and stimulated interest in trade with Asian countries.*

The Dutch East India Company *(V.O.C.) was the first multinational corporation worldwide and was founded in 1602 in order to strengthen Dutch tradesmen against the Portuguese, who had a monopoly in the spice trade, by working as a trade unit. The company was given special powers by the Dutch state such as the right to negotiate treaties, establish colonies and coin money. The trading centre was in Indonesia. Control of the trade route for spices from Indonesia to Europe resulted in the company's great success. In the 18th century the V.O.C., whose only competitor was the English East India Company (E.I.C.), went bankrupt and was formally dissolved in 1798.*

Lernwortschatz *era, Old World/New World, to shrink sth, agent, force, to drive sth, imperialism, competition, opportunity, to go global, to collaborate, the Great Depression, multinational company, stock, to power sth, falling costs, transportation costs, global economy, goods (pl), global market, to flatten sth, to empower sb/sth (to do sth), Western countries*

Materialien → CD, Track 2 • Online-Link: 601002-0001

Discussion **1 *When do you think globalisation really started?***

L beginnt mit der Wiederholung der Definition von Globalisierung. Weitere Fragestellungen: *Were goods, services and ideas exchanged? Which ones? Who benefited from Columbus's arrival in the Americas in the short term/long term?* Mögliche Zusammenfassung des Brainstormings: *Various stages of globalisation began with Marco Polo/Columbus/V.O.C./industrialisation. Goods and ideas were exchanged.*

Lösungsvorschlag *To answer the question when globalisation really started we have to ask ourselves what we connect with the term globalisation. On the one hand it is the modern phenomenon of different countries coming closer by easy ways of communication and transport. On the other hand early journeys like Columbus's trip to America can be seen as the beginning of globalisation. Therefore we should realise globalisation is not a development that started at a sudden point but should be seen as a process that started hundreds of years ago and is not yet finished. There were, however, various events in history that can be regarded as important parts of globalisation. As already mentioned journeys and exploration trips were the beginning of the exchange of goods and ideas. Industrialisation came, during which nations like England or Germany rose to become industrial powers, and was followed by inventions like airplanes. Through this transport became easier and importing and exporting began to dominate the worldwide economy. In modern times the invention of the Internet was a last step to complete globalisation as companies got rid off all barriers in communication. As mentioned above globalisation did not start at a certain point but can be seen as a result of different important developments in history.*

1 | Global challenges   The three eras of globalization

Research

2 When Columbus went to America, ...

Die S reflektieren über die Herkunft von Papier, Schießpulver und Kompass und geben ggf. weitere Informationen zu diesen Dingen. Ausführliche Infos zur Geschichte des Papiers: http://papiergeschichte.freyerweb.at/frueh.html.

Lösungsvorschlag

It is generally agreed that Columbus's journey to America was one of the most dangerous explorations in history. It was difficult enough to travel across the whole Atlantic Ocean and as we all know he did not know exactly where he was. However, the trip would have been impossible without taking a few things with him. Among others, paper, gunpowder and a compass were the most important. All these inventions made their way from China to Europe. For a long time these inventions were kept secret by the Chinese. Paper for example was already in use during the 6th century in China. It took about 400 years until paper reached Europe and was imported somewhere between the 10th and 11th century. It was the Chinese as well who invented the compass around 1100. Summing up, we realise that all the inventions that made Columbus successful came from China and were not of European origin.

Comparing pictures

3 Compare and contrast these two different interpretations ...

Die S beschreiben beide Bilder und befassen sich mit den Unterschieden, besonders mit der unterschiedlichen Darstellung von Kolumbus und den Eingeborenen. L: *Describe the pictures. Where is Columbus? How is he depicted (kneeling, standing, …)? Compare his stature and body language to those of the natives.*

Lösungsvorschlag

Left picture	*Right picture*
• *Columbus is kneeling, eyes towards God in heaven.*	• *Columbus is standing, determined.*
• *Religious symbols: cross, importance of religion.*	• *Today the cross would be replaced by a flag (see depiction of man planting cross and compare to moon landing).*
• *Natives are shy, hesitatant, still in the dark/ shadows and seem smaller than the Europeans.*	• *Natives are more in the foreground, bringing valuable presents.*
• *Columbus as grateful man, devoted to God.*	• *Columbus as dominant conquerer.*

Conclusion: The main difference in these two pictures is the way, Columbus is presented. The picture on the left shows him humble before God. Religion seems to play a big part in the success of his journey. Moreover, next to Columbus is a priest holding a cross to heaven. This underlines the importance of religion for Columbus's crew and his journey to America. In addition, the natives in the painting seem to be shy and stay in the background. The painting on the right, however, shows Columbus in a self-confident way as a dominant conqueror. Instead of the priest, Columbus is accompanied by two armoured soldiers. Although two workers are putting up a cross in the background, the painter pays more attention to the aspect of wealth than religion. Furthermore, the natives are not as shy as in the painting on the left. On the contrary, they are donating valuable presents to the invaders. One can conclude that the intention of these two paintings is different. The painter on the left tries to show how important religion was to Columbus. The other painter tries to underline how great Columbus's achievement was.

Alternative

• Die Aufgaben 1–3 werden als zusammenhängende **Hausaufgabe** gestellt und vor der Texterarbeitung besprochen.

[2◎]

• Erarbeitung des Textes mit der CD-ROM. L spielt **Track 2** vor und überprüft das Globalverstehen vor dem zweiten Vorspielen. Nach dem zweiten Hören wird das Detailverstehen anhand von Aufgabe 4 geprüft. Dazu *scanning* des Textes, um die nötigen Details aus den einzelnen Textabschnitten herauszusuchen.

Global challenges   The three eras of globalization   1

Visualising   ## 4 Find headings for the different parts of the text

Verweis auf *VIP file* zu Thomas L. Friedman. L: *What do you associate with the book's title "The World Is Flat"?* Mögliche Antwort: *"Flattening" of the world associated with belief in the Middle Ages that the world is flat.* Die S gestalten eine *mind-map* mit Hilfe der gefundenen Überschriften und präsentieren sie auf Folie oder Poster (DIN A3). L: *Explain your mind-map to a partner/the course.* Mögliche Symbole: *muscles, horsepower, telecommunication, S/M/L as for clothes.* Die *summary* in Aufgabe **b)** erfolgt mündlich oder als schriftliche **Hausaufgabe** anhand der *mind-map.*

Lösungsvorschlag   **a) Headings**
Globalisation 1.0: From a size large to a size medium:
"Countries struggling for more colonies"
Globalisation 2.0: From a size medium to a size small:
"Multinational companies struggling for more profit"
Globalisation 3.0: From a size small to a size tiny:
"Individuals from every corner of the world try to take part in the advantages of globalisation"

Keywords and symbols for mind-map
1.0:   imperialism, religion, global competition among countries, question about a country's brawn
2.0:   industrial revolution, multinational companies and global markets, railroad and steam engine as symbols, later: easy communication, global economy, PC, telephone and www as symbols
3.0:   global competition among individuals, different to the others: happens in mind, question about the individual's space in globalisation

b) *The text "The three eras of globalisation" suggests dividing the development of globalisation into three eras. According to the author's opinion a first era in globalisation can be seen in the time between Columbus's arrival in America and around 1800. During this time different countries and governments had to demonstrate their power in a global competition about colonies and resources.*
The second era is drawn from 1800 to the year 2000. This era again is divided into two parts. The first half of the second era can basically be called the time of industrialisation. Different inventions like the railway made transport easy and global markets possible. In the second half of this era communication between long distances became quite easy. Among a great number of inventions telephone, the PC and the Internet should be mentioned.
The third era started around the year 2000 and lasts until today. It is different from the first two eras as it mainly happened in people's minds. People started to wonder where their place in globalisation was and how they could profit from this development.

Visualising   ## 5 [👥] Do some research on one of the three eras.

Hinführung   L: *Comment on the two pictures in the text on page 7.* Mögliche Antwort: *The two pictures represent the different eras of globalisation. While in the second era the global competition among multinational companies like Shell dominated globalisation, a website like MySpace represents a new generation of Internet users who communicate via the web and take part in different Internet communities. Moreover, an oil refinery is a fitting image for the energy crisis that follows the excessive use of resources since the time of industrialisation. The whole world did not reflect on the consequences. Building up second identities on Internet platforms seems for some people to be a new way to cope with a loss of identity. This is what the author mentions about globalisation 3.0 as a development taking place in people's minds. Both images are therefore on the one hand representative of their era, on the other hand critical images about the possible results of this global development.*

Erarbeitung   Die S suchen sich eine der drei im Text beschriebenen Zeitalter aus und sammeln darüber Informationen (Internetrecherche in der Schule oder als **Hausaufgabe**). Anschließend

13

1 Global challenges The three eras of globalization

gestalten sie mit diesen Informationen entweder einen Zeitstrahl, eine *Fact file* oder ein Plakat. Die Gruppenarbeitsergebnisse werden im Plenum präsentiert.

Lösungsvorschlag

Era 1.0: Timeline (detailed with background information)

1275	Marco Polo reaches Beijing and meets Kublai Khan.
1419	Portugal sends ships to explore the African coast with the aim of finding a route for trading spice with Asia.
1444	The first slaves from Mauritania are brought to Portugal.
1452	Pope Nicholas V allows Portugal to make pagans their slaves.
1492	Christopher Columbus discovers America.
1500	Pedro Álvares Cabral founds the colony of Brazil for Portugal.
1555	John Lok is the first Briton to take slaves from Africa to England.
1602	The Dutch East India Company (V.O.C./Verenigde Oostindische Compagnie) is founded.
1603	The V.O.C. establishes its first trading post in Indonesia in Banten, West Java.
1605	The French found their first colony, Acadia in North America (today's Nova Scotia, Canada).
1606	V.O.C. is the first company to issue stock.
1606	The British East India Company is founded.
1608	Samuel de Champlain founds the French fur trading colony, Quebec.
1624	France establishes its first trading posts in Senegal.
1652	The V.O.C. establishes outposts in Persia, Bengal, Malacca, Siam, China, Formosa and southern India. In addition, the largest Dutch colony, Cape Colony at the Cape of Good Hope, is established by Jan van Riebeeck.
1664	The French East India Company is founded, establishing colonies in Île de la Réunion in the Indian Ocean.
1706/1707	The Acts of Union are passed by British Parliament, uniting the Kingdom of Scotland with the Kingdom of England.
1712	The first steam engine is built by Thomas Newcomen in England.
1718	France makes Mauritius its colony.
1727	The term "sustainability" is first used in an English document.
1729	Chinese government bans opium.
1756	France turns the Seychelles into its colony.
1756–1763	The Seven Years War involves all major European powers. The war ends with the Treaty of 1763 and the dominance of Britain in India as well as the loss of French settlements in the Americas.
1770	James Cook discovers Botany Bay (Australia).
1776	Thomas Jefferson writes the Declaration of Independence. It is a list of grievances against the King in order to justify before the world the breaking of ties between the 13 colonies in America and Britain.
1781	Britain imports to China large amounts of opium from India.
1787	The first steamboat, built by John Fitch in Pennsylvania, obtains a patent.

Era 2.0: Timeline/Fact box

Late 18th, beginning 19th century:	Industrial Revolution starts in England. Inventions like steam machine, followed by the first railways made way for higher production in factories and cheaper transport.
19th century:	Invention of telegraph and later the telephone lead to falling communication costs.
1914–1918:	World War I interrupts the development of globalisation.
1920–1929:	The Golden Twenties, time of economic successes.
1929:	Black Tuesday as the beginning of the great depression, time of economic downturn, setting stage for World War II.
1939–1945:	World War II as another break in progress of global integration.
20th century:	Invention of the PC and early forms of the www. Birth of global economy.

Global challenges **Spot on facts** | **1**

Era 3.0: Fact box
Globalisation 3.0 is no longer a matter of industrial changes and new inventions but a general change in thinking. Individuals from all over the world begin to think globally and try to take part and use the advantages of globalisation. The development of globalisation is a generally accepted progress driven by diverse groups of individuals from every corner of the world. There is no longer a dominance of white people from western countries over the rest of the world. China and India are being empowered. Their influence on the global economy will significantly increase in the next decades.

Text production | ## 6 *Creative writing*

Verweis auf Kasten mit *Useful phrases* zu *Individual opportunities*. Stichwörter, die die S bei ihren Ausarbeitungen berücksichtigen können: *use of technology/the Internet in daily life; access to global information; parents' flexibility (change of residence, job); international school projects; internships/studying abroad.*

Lösungsvorschlag | *Globalisation means a lot of pressure to today's individuals. This starts at early age at school when young children have to learn foreign languages and compete against others as this is compulsory in modern societies. We are, however, taking part in globalisation without being aware of it. Using the Internet and visiting international websites, taking part in international student exchanges are everyday aspects of globalisation we might not realise. So we don't even have the chance to decide whether we want to take part in the global competition, but everyone is already doing it. This does not matter as in many cases taking part in globalisation does not involve any risks. A lot of people in modern societies, however, suffer from the pressure of disappearing opportunities and from multinational influences getting more complicated. Life is getting harder and people's living standards are closely connected to the international economy, but the majority of people are able to agree with the global standards. Although globalisation does not only provoke positive reactions it offers many favourable opportunities to all of us. A lot of people are given the chance to earn a living in foreign countries, collaborating with people from different continents and above all nearly everyone uses the easy ways of communicating and travelling. Thus I as an individual take part in the global competition and do not forego the opportunities globalisation offers.*

Factual
information
Lernwortschatz | ## Spot on facts   p. 8

globalisation, technological, mobility, refugee, flow, production site, to increase, spread, value, distribution, global player, multinational (company), labour, overhead costs, to expand, to cut costs, efficiency, profit, working hours, wages (pl), condition, unemployment, retirement, demand, qualification, decade, advance, electronics (sg), revolution, to aid, branch, to preserve, income, human rights (pl), peaceful, universal, prosperity, ecological, stability, dependence, support, investment, credit, mass medium, media (pl), to predict, means (sg or pl), ethnic tension, pollution, competitive, gap

Discussion | ## 1 *What conditions were necessary for globalisation ...*

Zusatzmaterial | → Kopiervorlage 1 (Global values/Global challenges)

Lösungsvorschlag | *The fast progress of communication technologies such as the Internet was crucial for the development of globalisation and has led to a global spread of ideas and values (l. 11: microelectronics revolution, l. 19: advances in communication technologies). The increased exchange of money and goods between international markets and production sites prepared the groundwork for a growing global market (l. 18: global economic activity).*

Erweiterung | Zur Vertiefung bietet sich hier der Einsatz von **Kopiervorlage 1** (Seite 93) an. Das Arbeitsblatt enthält themenbezogene Raster als Diskussionsgrundlagen für eine Partnerarbeitsphase.

15

1 Global challenges The corporation

Discussion **2 What are your personal hopes and fears ...**

Zusatzmaterial → Kopiervorlage 2 (Globalisation – definitions)

Zu den Gefahren bzw. Ängsten kann L folgende Hinweise geben: *People have to move away from home, no job due to outsourcinig, too much flexibility required.*

Lösungsvorschlag *Globalisation is accompanied by many advantages. The possibilities for young people are enormous and the use of the Internet to visit multinational websites is part of daily life. Therefore we have to regard ourselves as part of globalisation. But still, everyone of us has hopes and fears we have to consider while talking about globalisation. We all hope that the advantages of globalisation will help us some day. Jobs in multinational companies are in demand, studying in foreign countries is getting interesting for every young student and a safe global economy is important for our personal living standards.*
On the other hand, every day European companies dismiss workforces in order to produce more cheaply in Third World countries and make higher profits. Hardly any job in the economy and industry is really safe and employees are under great pressure. The current trends of globalisation must be seen in different ways. Either they offer you great international possibilities or they lead to a high number of unemployed people. The gap between the poor and the rich is increasing and no one can offer reasonable solutions.

Erweiterung Zum Abschluss dieses Abschnitts kann **Kopiervorlage 2** (Seite 94) eingesetzt werden. Das Arbeitsblatt enthält eine weitere Definition des Begriffes *Globalisation* zum Vergleich.

Video clip **[🎬] The corporation** p. 9

HINTERGRUNDINFO

The corporation: This documentary examines the nature and rise of the corporation, the most dominant institution of our time. Along with the analysis of its history and present manifestations, Mark Achbar, producer and director of "The corporation", has also included interviews with 40 corporate insiders and critics. Based on Joel Bakan's book "The Corporation: The Pathological Pursuit of Profit and Power", the film was a great success and received numerous awards. "The Corporation" is one of the most successful Canadian feature documentaries ever made. Prominent people appearing in the film clip include: Joe Badaracco, professor of business ethics at Harvard Business School, and Joel Bakan, eminent Canadian law professor, legal theorist and author of the book "The Corporation".

Lernwortschatz corporation, relatively insignificant, all-pervasive, to trigger, basic operating principles, the corporate world, CEO, a bunch of bad apples, a crisis of confidence, a common purpose, hard to avoid, artificial creation, to devour, at anyone's expense, agenda

Materialien → Film, Track 1 • Online-Link: 601002-0002

Pre-viewing activity **1 Before viewing**

[🎬] Die S finden eine Definition von *corporation*, auch als **Hausaufgabe** möglich. Die Ergebnisse werden im Kursgespräch verglichen. Danach wird **Track 1** von der CD-ROM präsentiert.

Lösungsvorschlag *A large company or business organisation.*
Artificial creation, association of people.
Business group of individuals working together to serve a variety of objectives, the principal one of which is earning large, growing, sustained, legal returns for the people who own the business.
Grew out of the industrial age.
Limited liability (Ltd. = BE); Incorporated (Inc. = AE)

Erweiterung Die S werden aufgefordert, die Rolle von Großkonzernen im Prozess der Globalisierung nachzuvollziehen (siehe **Online-Link**).

16

Global challenges **The corporation** | **1**

| Post-viewing activity | **2 [åå] *What associations do you have for ...*** |

Die S schreiben ihre Assoziationen mit dem Wort *apple* auf und erstellen eine Liste oder legen eine *mind-map* an. Letztere bietet den Vorteil, dass sie sich gut ergänzen und visualisieren lässt.

Lösungsvorschlag *Apple Macintosh, the iPod and iPhone company, vitamins/healthy, Adam's apple, the Big Apple (NYC), toffee apple, candy apple (AE), apple tree, apple orchard, etc.*

| Post-viewing activity | **3 *After viewing*** |

L: *What is a whistle blower?* Mögliche Antwort: *Heroes who help uncover crimes, or traitors who betray their company or government department.* Hinweis zum kritischen Charakter der Dokumentation: *How often do you think whistle blowers face negative consequences at work?*

Lösungsvorschlag *The beginning of this documentary attracts attention at once. A great number of corporation labels are shown in rapid succession. All of these pictures are well known from TV commercials everyone knows even without understanding the term "corporation" – the subject of the documentary.*
On the other hand it is difficult to keep focused on the text as the fast succession of images competes for the audience's attention. A documentary should not only attract visually but also inform about the topic. Although one might be interested by many popular brands and logos the film appears at the beginning to be more a commercial than a documentary.

Erweiterung Auftrag für eine Gruppenarbeitsphase: *Carry out a short interview in your course and show the results in a chart: If you observed serious wrongdoing at your school or in your community, do you think you would become a whistle blower?* Die S präsentieren Säulen-/Tortendiagramm (*yes/no/don't know*) auf Folie.

| Discussion | **4 *What is the term 'bad apples' used for?*** |

Lösungsvorschlag *The term is used for corporations/their managements that are guilty of serious wrongdoing. Message: From the outside I may look wrong/bad, but I'm still a nice person/attractive (see other songs, e.g. Alanis Morissette, The Osmonds, Aaron Carter).*

| Note-taking | **5 *List the images used to describe the corporation*** |

Die S schauen den Filmausschnitt zum zweiten Mal an. L: *Watch out! The sequences follow each other very fast. Take down notes about the images.* Die S schreiben die verschiedenen Bilder auf, die für den Begriff *corporation* gebraucht werden, und tauschen sich darüber aus. Die positiven und negativen Konnotationen werden besprochen.

Lösungsvorschlag
1. *a jigsaw puzzle (only working as a whole)*
2. *a sports team (some blocking and tackling, some are running and throwing the ball)*
3. *a family unit (working together for a common end)*
4. *the telephone system (reaching everywhere, powerful and hard to avoid)*
5. *the eagle (soaring, clear-eyed, noble, a visionary, creates a lift, prepared to strike)*
6. *artificial creations, monsters (to devour, Frankenstein's monster has overpowered his creator)*
7. *a whale (gentle big fish, but can swallow you in an instant)*
8. *agenda, strategy*

| Analysis | **6 *Give examples of how the film's message is enhanced*** |

L: *Add cinematic devices (as named in the task) next to your previous notes and comment on their effect on the viewer/you.* Mögliche Hilfestellung: *People at work in office and bird's-eye*

17

1 Global challenges Sourcing global talent in software

view of doll house, opening credits, brand names and voice-over, images for corporations and film excerpts (black & white), medium shots of commentators, etc.

Lösungsvorschlag *Fast cuts between modern pictures in colour and the montages of old black and white images show how fast the development of corporations has been in the last 150 years. It used to be institutions like the church or the monarchy that dominated people's lives. They are represented by short interruptions as black and white pictures. Today it is, however, the corporation shown by various pictures in colour that has taken over this part. Fruit (i.e. apple) and animals (i.e. eagle, whale) are used as symbols carrying the message that the development of corporations is dangerous for people all over the world. The sound and the captions underline the general message of the documentary.*

Evaluation **7 In the German subtitles, 'corporation' is translated ...**

Vergleich mit den Definitionen in Aufgabe 1.

Lösungsvorschlag *To answer this question we have to examine the exact meaning of the different German terms. The German expression "Konzern" for example is the amalgamation of different companies. All of these companies work together and are, however, legally independent. The main company of this amalgamation is the so called "parent company", the others work as subsidiary companies. As well as a "Konzern" "Kapitalgesellschaft" is more a legal term than an explanation of the size and profit of a company. Although Germans use "Großunternehmen" and "Konzern" or "Kapitalgesellschaft" often in similar ways, the definitions above show that there are significant differences. Summing up the term "Konzern" as an amalgamation of different companies seems to offer the best definition of the way the corporation is explained in the documentary.*

Discussion **8 If corporations were persons, which characteristics ...**

Verweis auf Useful phrases *zu* Talking about characteristics. L: *Which corporations do you know?* Evtl. kurzer Austausch in Partnerarbeit. Mögliche Antwort: *In the documentation corporations are defined as legal persons.* L: *Which characteristics would you give those corporations? Compare your findings with a partner and report back to the course giving short descriptions of the corporations.*

Lösungsvorschlag
- *Chrysler – fast, reliable.*
- *Nike – athletic, young, energetic.*
- *Microsoft – clever, sly, savvy, useful.*
- *McDonalds – omnipresent, young, fast, outgoing.*
- *Disney – goofy, silly, childish, funny, entertaining.*
- *The Body Shop – organic, deceptive, lovely.*

Erweiterung Anregung für *discussion* oder *comment writing: Social responsibility and accountability: Choose one of the corporations named in the documentary and discuss whether it acts ethically and socially responsibly.*

Interview **[3◉] Sourcing global talent in software** pp. 10/11

HINTERGRUNDINFO

*Professor **Dr. Henning Kagermann** (b. 1947), German physicist and manager of SAP, started his career in 1982 and became a member of the SAP AG's board of directors in 1991. Seven years later the professor of theoretical physics accepted the post of chief executive. In April 2008 he confirmed his plan to retire in spring 2009.*

*The German company **SAP AG** is the biggest software producer in Europe and ranks third on the global market. It was founded more than 35 years ago in Walldorf/Germany. Today, SAP employs about 44,000 people in over 50 countries. The company's focus is on software development for small, medium and large enterprises.*

Global challenges   Sourcing global talent in software   1

Silicon Valley is located south of the San Francisco Bay Area in Northern California. Associated with the high-tech sector, it is home to many international companies like Google, Apple Inc., Hewlett Packard, and Yahoo. Silicon Valley is the leading high-tech hub in the US. The term "Silicon Valley" originates from the region's large number of silicon chip innovators and manufacturers and was first used in a newspaper article in 1971.

Palo Alto is a town located at the northern end of Silicon Valley, where several of the high-tech companies have their headquarters. It is also home to Stanford University.

Lernwortschatz sourcing, independence, transformation, world (market) leader, competition, transition, smoothly, to tap (into) sth, pool, specific knowledge; deep knowledge, innovation, creativity, gradually, high-quality products

Materialien → CD, Track 3

Survey **1 How many people in your class want to become scientists, ...**

[3◉] Nach der Bearbeitung von Aufgabe 1 wird der Text entweder in Stillarbeit gelesen oder L spielt **Track 3** von der CD-ROM vor.

Lösungsvorschlag The motivation to become a scientist, computer specialist or engineer is easy to point out. All of these jobs are in a great demand. Good marks in exams in one of these fields are equal to a job guarantee. They all fit in to multinational companies and the possibility to get offered a job in a foreign country is quite good. These fields belong arguably to those on which globalisation has had the most positive effect. Furthermore, the chances of a good salary are high. But still, the motivation to study one of these difficult subjects should have some connection with personal interests and talents. People who are not interested in mathematics, physics or other sciences should not think about a job in one of these fields. This could be the reason why many people are not interested in one of these important and much sought-after jobs.

Making a map **2 Create a world map of SAP's operations ...**

Lösungsvorschlag The largest number of SAP workers are in Germany (two-thirds of the total number of workers); then about 3,000 in India; 1,400 in Palo Alto, California; 1,000 in China; 900 in Israel and the remaining thousands spread among about 45 other countries. Germany's engineers are responsible for deep application integration (finance, manufacturing, human relations, etc.). In Palo Alto a lot of the Internet work is done that opens SAP's products to other people. India has been responsible for much of the design work so far.

Discussion **3 Outline how SAP makes use of outsourcing.**

Lösungsvorschlag The chief executive of SAP mentions a very important point of outsourcing. He underlines that a worldwide company like SAP can not only use talents from one country but has to make use of the best engineers from all over the world. Therefore SAP has moved one third of its engineering work into countries like India, China and Israel. Especially in India there is a large number of talented software specialists. In Silicon Valley, California, however, they try to work on new inventions and ideas. A lot of worldwide companies are located in Silicon Valley and global integration is quite easy there. Still, the main work is done in Germany. According to Henning Kagermann "the basic architecture of the core product" is done there as SAP needs the knowledge of German engineers. In conclusion one could explain the reasons SAP outsources with the increasing demand in worldwide talents in computer software and engineering. SAP uses the human resources available in the various countries where it outsources. The company takes advantage of the special carabilities of the workers in Germany, India, China, the US and other countries.

1 Global challenges Cartooning outsourcing

Text production   **4 Creative writing**

Lösungsvorschlag   *Dear Ladies and Gentlemen,*
The interview with the chief executive of SAP in the "New York Times" attracted my interest in engineering and software work. I have almost finished school and have been wondering what to study for a long time. Therefore I do not understand why big companies like SAP do not offer programmes at schools to attract more young people to doing these jobs. As we all know, Germany has a shortage of engineers. Isn't it in the interest of global companies like SAP to eradicate this problem? I think the responsibility of these companies to attract young people and find talents is enormous. Therefore, I think companies like SAP should invest more in school programmes, offer young people industrial placements and do publicity for engineering work. Furthermore, they could offer young software students holiday jobs in order to offer perspectives and insights in a worldwide company and possible future jobs. I earnestly hope you will take my suggestions seriously and you will be able to attract more young people to start a study with an engineering background.
Sincerely yours,

Cartoons

Cartooning outsourcing   p. 11

Discussion   **1 Look at the cartoons and discuss the pros and cons ...**

Lösungsvorschlag

Pros	Cons
• Wealth is spread among the working people of the world. • Talented people are able to make use of their gifts.	• There is less work for some people in traditionally good companies. • People acquire the attitude that any type of work that is not fun can and should be outsourced to be done by people with fewer choices than they.

Magazine article

Moving goods around the globe   pp. 12/13

HINTERGRUNDINFO

*When **cargo** was still loaded by hand, factories were located in the vicinity of harbours in order to save transport costs and speed up the delivery process. The introduction of the shipping container allowed faster and more efficient transportation. As a consequence, there was a movement away from the busy city ports to cheaper locations. Today there is a similar movement going on as factories try to be as close to airports as possible. Thus, they can take orders until very late in the evening and still send their goods around the globe the same night. An example for such an industrial centre is Frankfurt Airport City (search keyword on the Internet is "Fraport").*

***Kuehne+Nagel** is one of the world's leading logistics providers, founded in Bremen/Germany in 1890. With more than 51,000 employees working in 830 offices in 100 countries, the company offers services including sea freight, airfreight, rail and road logistics and contract logistics.*

***DHL** is an acronym standing for the three founders' surnames Dalsey, Hillblom and Lynn. It is a Deutsche Post company offering inter- national shipping of documents and freight as well as contract logistics (see also **Hintergrundinfo**, p. 8).*

***FedEx (Federal Express)** Corporation was founded in 1971 by Fred Smith in Little Rock, Arkansas. It is one of the leading logistics services companies with its headquarters in Memphis, Tennessee. The global network of companies that are united under the name FedEx provide specialised services including supply chains, transportation, business and related information services.*

***UPS (United Parcel Service Inc.)** was founded in 1907 as a messenger company in the US. UPS became one of the largest express carrier and package delivery company worldwide and aims to advance the development of the flows of goods, information and funds.*

Global challenges Moving goods around the globe   1

Lernwortschatz *warehouse, efficiency, supply chain, supply, to improve sth, goods (pl), containerisation, dramatic, to flourish, to be the world's leader/world market leader in sth, freight forwarder, to operate, contract, on land, at sea, in the air, to consolidate, modes of transport, range, to deliver, to expand, to capitalise on sth, to make an investment*

Presentation   ## 1 Why was the invention of the container revolutionary?

L: *What do you know about containers?* Die S präsentieren eine kurze Zusammenfassung der Ergebnisse in der Klasse.

Lösungsvorschlag *First of all one has to mention that by the invention of the container the number of goods that could be transported together escalated. The easy way of packing these square boxes made it easy to pack more goods together. As a result the shipping industry could transport more goods on one ship. Containers can be stacked without wasting space. Moreover, it is now usual to unload the containers from a ship and directly load them onto a truck. Fewer goods get lost, broken or damaged in any way as the containers can easily be transported on water, but also by train, truck or airplane. A multinational and uniform system of transporting containers developed and made it easy for transport and logistic companies to work together.*
For these reasons the invention of the container was revolutionary and another step into a multinational economic system, which can basically be described by the term globalisation. Containers make the transport of goods faster, easier and cheaper: they reduce costs.

Analysis   ## 2 Describe what services K+N offers ...

L: *What does the chart tell you about the container market?* Mögliche Antwort: *Graph chart showing growing container market; symbol ship; rising graph.* L bietet als Ergänzung zur Grafik *The way to go* (Seite 13 oben) folgendes Zitat von Michael Frenzel (TUI CEO): *"Container shipping is one of the last major growth frontiers of globalisation."* (Spiegel special, 2005).

Lösungsvorschlag
- *Seaborne, ground transport.*
- *Arranges for other companies' goods to be transported by other ships.*
- *Large-scale air-freight forwarder.*
- *Operates road and rail services.*
- *Growing demand for integrated and specialised services.*
- *Container shipping industry is booming.*

Analysis   ## 3 Use the information in the text ...

L-Impuls: *Explain the meaning of the following statement: "Containers are the building blocks of the global village."* Mögliche Erklärung: *Growing demand and increasing division of labour and markets (China and Europe as the world's manufacturers, US its main consumers) demands quick and reliable transport.*

Lösungsvorschlag *K+N does not offer any transport services itself. They arrange the transport for several companies. Globalisation opened opportunities for services like the ones K+N offers, which operates in many countries. They work together with many other different companies in all fields of business. On the one hand they need companies to produce goods, on the other they work together with transport companies like UPS. All these companies are located in different countries and goods have to be transported from one continent to another. K+N's profit strategy is based on international relations and globalisation. UPS, however, makes profit as big companies outsource different services to the former delivery company. Nowadays UPS does not only deliver goods from one place to another. Globalisation offered the possibility to work hand in hand with technical companies like Toshiba for example.*

1 Global challenges — Frischer Wind für Frachter

Discussion **4 Explain the importance of the observation: …**

Lösungsvorschlag The competition will have to work with containers (boxes), too. It is the most effective way of transporting goods. Outsourced products/parts must reach their final destination safely and cheaply.

Evaluation **5 Presentation**

Verweis auf *Useful phrases* zu *Presenting a statement*. Die S tragen Argumente aus den vorhergehenden Aufgaben zusammen und arbeiten kurze *statements* aus. Einige S tragen ihre Überlegungen vor, es folgt eine Diskussion in der Klasse.

Lösungsvorschlag
- Globalisation requires increased co-ordination of transport by road, rail, sea and air.
- One kind of transportation is as bad environmentally as the other – no alternatives.
- Even "German" products are made in several parts of the world (outsourcing), so we don't have a choice.

Text production **6 Put the information of the last paragraph …**

Je nach Zielstellung mündliche oder schriftliche Textproduktion (evtl. als **Hausaufgabe**). L gibt zusätzlichen Hinweis: *UPS uses the phrase "Synchronising the world of commerce".*

Lösungsvorschlag **General global context**
- Competition in the logistics/supply chain business is fierce.
- Exploration of new fields.
- Sourcing of services into the company surely is a trend.

Comment: UPS used to be a "messenger and delivery service in Seattle" (l. 47/48). Nowadays they not only deliver goods worldwide but also offer other different services. The example given in the text is a repair shop for laptops which is run by UPS in cooperation with Toshiba. This cannot be seen as a development concerning only UPS but seems to be a worldwide trend of globalisation. Companies grow together, outsource different services to other companies and transport and logistic companies start to build up new businesses.
A company that wants to work multinationally has to adapt to this global development by being quite flexible and offer new services. Big companies buy smaller companies and the worldwide economy grows together. The difficulty with this development is that every country is losing its economic independence to the global economy. Third World countries are more dependent on the big industrial nations and a small economic crisis can lead to a global downturn in the economy and living standards. Also when considering all the positive effects of globalisation this trend should be regarded as quite troubling.

Magazine article **Frischer Wind für Frachter** p. 14

HINTERGRUNDINFO

SkySails started in 2001 with the development of a towing kite system, for which it is famous since it was the first of its kind worldwide. Six years later the first system was installed on freighters, of which the "Beluga SkySails" was the first. In 2008, after a successful testing period, the company began with the serial production of the towing kite system. Stephan Wrage (born 1972) is the founder of SkySails and chairman of the management board.

Lernwortschatz freighter, (towing) kite, sail, power, to set sail, fuel costs, shipping company, adequate, wind power, to be dependent on, curious, to reduce sth by, environmentally friendly, additional, emission, climate, greenhouse gases (pl), development, to be worth it, break-even point

Materialien → Online-Link: 601002-0003

Global challenges   My global mind | **1**

Text production | **1 [👥] Mediation**

L: *Read the text and take notes of the most interesting facts (according to the given task) in English. Together think about what the American reporter would be likely to ask and write down the questions. If you need more information, go to the SkySails website. Carry out the interview with your partner.* Der anschließende Bericht erfolgt in Einzelarbeit: *Write a short report summarising the facts of your interview.*

Lösungsvorschlag | **Interview** *(mögliche Antworten in Klammern):*
Reporter: Could you explain the idea of SkySails more concretely? How exactly do you move the big container ships? (big kites in the air, wind strong enough to move ships)
Reporter: Wasn't it difficult to convince investors of your ideas? (very difficult, people doubted that it could work, now they are surprised and big companies are afraid of our success)
Reporter: When will the test trips be finished and SkySails offer its ideas to the industry? (cannot be sure about that, trying to get things ready as soon as possible)
Reporter: What do you expect for the future of SkySails? (success in shipping industry, therefore reducing the greenhouse effect and pollution)

Report: *Increasing amount of transport by planes, ships and trucks has led to serious environmental problems. The greenhouse effect and the expansion of the hole in the ozone layer are well known problems. Therefore we all have to work together in reducing energy waste. In the shipping industry the company SkySails seems to have found a solution for this development. Despite the doubts of experts, they move container ships using big kites and without wasting energy. After a long testing period they seem to be ready to offer the idea to transport companies. In future SkySails hopes to be quite successful in this business and thereby reduce environmental pollution.*

Erweiterung | *Find out about the operation of the system. Discuss it with people from a physics course and report back to the class what they think about it. As ships are already sailing with the system, do some research on their actual effectiveness.*

American song | **[4◎] My global mind**   p. 15

HINTERGRUNDINFO

Queensrÿche: Although they were initially grouped in with the legions of pop-metal bands that dominated the American heavy metal scene of the 1980s, Queensrÿche were one of the most distinctive bands of the era. Where their contemporaries built

on the legacy of Van Halen, Aerosmith, and Kiss, Queensrÿche constructed a progressive form of heavy metal that drew equally from the guitar pyrotechnics of post-Van Halen metal and 1970s art rock, most notably Pink Floyd and Queen.

Lernwortschatz | *assembly line, at the touch of a button, to reach out for sth, to hold sb/sth back, balance, to search for sth, to zero in on sth, attention span, information age*

Materialien | → CD, Track 4

Text production | **1 Try to describe what the singer is looking for ...**

[4◎] | Bevor Aufgabe 1 bearbeitet wird, spielt L **Track 4** zweimal von der CD-ROM vor.

Lösungsvorschlag | *The singer's feeling of helplessness is caused by the overwhelming effect globalisation has on the individual. As globalisation is a very fast and powerful phenomenon, people are not able to escape it. There is no protection (l. 40: No boundary's gonna keep it from you) and because of the Internet people can be found wherever they are (l. 36: It's searching everywhere). For the singer the Internet is just an escape (l. 3: At the touch of a button/I'm miles away) but no solution to hunger, poverty and to those people who "drown in the changes" (l. 12): globalisation*

23

1 Global challenges   My global mind

does not mean improvement for the poor but is rather considered a standstill or even a miserable situation regarding their lives. The singer wants globalisation to be a chance for everyone (l. 1/2: There's hunger in Africa/And anger on assembly lines).

Analysis

2 Find the metaphors in the song …

Lösungsvorschlag
- At the touch of a button/I'm miles away (l. 3/4)/turn my gaze to another place (l. 7/8): make the listener feel that it is easily possible to escape from reality.
- Wave/drown (l. 11/12): gives the listener the sense of being overwhelmed, that the world is turning too fast, and that destruction and death is at hand.
- Experience the flight (l. 14): gives the listener the freedom to feel that he/she is above things, that he/she can change perspectives, and be open to others' views.

Comparing songs

3 Compare the music and the message of this song to …

Lösungsvorschlag

	Globalisation Blues	My Global Mind
Globalisation is …	… a threat, overwhelming the individual and leaving him/her "dead".	… a danger, a "wave" that runs over people.
Tone of song	negative, but still hopeful, call to fight against it (cf. last stanza)	negative
Language	aggressive	not aggressive
Music	blues: express sadness, longing, slow, minor key	drums: more aggressive, harder rhythm, many stops, percussion
Rhetorical figures	addresses the listener ("you"), repetition	repetition, metaphors
Message	Take your chance on globalisation: fight back, do not let globalisation overwhelm you.	There is no escape from globalisation. It will find everyone and have an effect on people (you!) everywhere.

Evaluation

4 Write a definition of Information Age …

Lösungsvorschlag

Definition: The Information Age is marked by the rapid distribution of news through the media. More and more people around the globe gain access to information due to the fast development of communication technologies. As a result, the perception of time and space is changing.

Comment: The term "Information Age" refers to the present and remains in a close connection with globalisation. In contrast to the Industrial Age we have to realise that during recent years the global economy has no longer been dominated by the production of industrial goods. The business with modern information technologies like the Internet has become one of the most successful opportunities for companies and employers. Furthermore, Information Age means that people are confronted with a great variety of information by all kinds of media: TV, radio, newspapers and recently the Internet supply people with completely different points of view. It is very difficult to figure out what can be taken seriously.
Information Age is our era. We have not been confronted with other eras and it is therefore hard to compare it to other ages in history. Recent developments seem to be alarming. Countrys' populations are manipulated by the media and the Internet is not only an easy way of making a profit. Information technologies offer possibilities like outsourcing. Third World countries are still

Global challenges   Is American culture 'American'?   **1**

exhausted and their populations abused as cheap workforces for industrial countries. The Information Age should therefore not be condemned but be seen from a critical point of view.

| *Scholarly article* | **Is American culture 'American'?** | **pp. 16/17** |

HINTERGRUNDINFO

Richard Pells *is a professor of history at the University of Texas in Austin. He specialised in 20th century American culture and intellectual history. His current interest is the global impact of American culture and how foreign cultures have affected the United States. He is the author of three books: "Radical Visions and American Dreams: Culture and Social Thought in the Depression Years", "The Liberal Mind in a Conservative Age: American Intellectuals in the 1940s and 1950s", "Not Like Us: How Europeans Have Loved, Hated, and Transformed American Culture Since World War II". He often writes for newspapers and magazines, including the "International Herald Tribune", the "Los Angeles Times", and the "Chronicle of Higher Education". Pells received a Ph.D. from Harvard in 1969 and has taught in Amsterdam, Copenhagen, Bonn, Berlin, Cologne, and Vienna.*

Lernwortschatz   *to consume, immigrant, melting pot, to win sb over, impact, tradition, unique, identity, to persist, to loathe, to insist (on sth), allegation, one-sided, to spread, to incorporate, global mass/youth culture, decade, essential (to), concise, thus (fml), to be suited to sth, demand, ethnic diversity, medium (media, pl), to appeal to sb, technique, intrusive, to embrace, the Middle East, cosmopolitan, dependence, advertising, commercial, mutual, domestic, to transcend divisions*

Hinführung   *Pre-teach vocabulary if necessary: apprehension, loathe, eccentricities, disseminate, allegation, intrusive, compelling, resurgence.*

Pre-reading activity   **1 [👥] *What was there in Europe before ...***

Nach dem Austausch von Ideen in Partnerarbeit folgt ein kurzes Kursgespräch zum Vergleich der Ergebnisse.

Lösungsvorschlag   *McDonald's: snack bar* (Currywurst o.ä.), *home-cooking, lunch-box.*
Starbucks (relatively new in Germany, since 2001 in Berlin): Kaffee und Kuchen, *mostly at home, sometimes at café.*
Hollywood: UFA, DEFA (Babelsberg), *German stars* (Heinz Rühmann, Marlene Dietrich u.a.).
Disneyland: country fairs, circus, pleasure parks (e.g. Hansapark), Weihnachtsmarkt.

Pre-reading activity   **2 [👥] *With a partner, find a definition of culture ...***

Kurzes Kursgespräch zum Zusammentragen der Ergebnisse: *What associations do you have with American culture? Refer to the picture on page 16.*

Lösungsvorschlag   *Culture is a set of ideas, beliefs, values and knowledge that is shared by a social community. It has no fixed boundaries and is not static. Culture is manifested in activities and ideas, which often refer to common traditions, of a group of people and can be articulated through music, literature, lifestyle, painting, theatre and many other similar things.*

Comprehension   **3 *Summarise the main points of each paragraph ...***

Die S fassen die zentralen Aussagen in Einzelarbeit zusammen (evtl. als **Hausaufgabe**). Der Vergleich der Antworten erfolgt über eine von L oder S vorbereitete Folie.

25

1 | Global challenges   Is American culture 'American'?

Lösungsvorschlag

	Main points
lines 1–7, 1st paragraph	Since at least 1901, people around the world have been afraid of Americanisation.
2nd paragraph	Trend toward cultural uniformity, American culture destroys regional and local customs/specialties.
3rd paragraph	Cultural relationship between America and the world went in two directions.
4th paragraph	Thanks to immigrants, foreign cultures were incorporated into American culture and reappeared as a unique feature.
5th paragraph	What is considered American culture today was not invented there.
6th paragraph	The effectiveness of English has helped the acceptance and spread of American mass culture.
7th paragraph	Because of its population diversity, American culture has always had a multicultural appeal.
8th paragraph	America's mass culture transformed what it received from other cultures and made it its own.
9th paragraph	That's why the US is a copy of the cultures of the world.

Erweiterung   Schriftliche **Hausaufgabe**: *Write a summary of this text using no more than 150 words.*

Analysis   ## 4 *Analyse how the author uses words with negative connotations ...*

Verweis auf *Useful phrases* zu *Analysing a text*. Rhetorische Mittel erkennen und funktionalisieren. Die S benennen der entsprechenden Wörter und erklären deren Effekt.

Lösungsvorschlag   *l. 2: ... uncomfortable with the global impact of American culture.*
l. 3: ... ominously, The Americanisation of the World.
l. 4: ... apprehensions.
ll. 5/6: ... obliteration of a country's unique identity under the weight of American habits ...
ll. 9/10: ... loathe what they see as the trend toward cultural uniformity.
l. 12: ... eradicating regional and local eccentricities.
ll. 18/19: ... shaper of the world's entertainment and tastes.

Effect: *Rather negative connotations with American culture and the role it plays in the world. Prepares the foundation for the positive arguments that follow in the next part of the text and the conclusion.*

Presentation   ## 5 *Giving a speech*

L: *How difficult did you find this text? What aspects made it difficult?* Mögliche Antwort: *The text is rather difficult because of the formal style (sophisticated choice of words, unknown to most pupils).* Die Aufgabe ist auch in Partnerarbeit möglich: *Work with a partner and rewrite the text using a more casual style. What would be your first step? Give your speech in class.*

Lösungsvorschlag   *Main ideas*
On the one hand:
- *a general opinion among academics about the Americanisation of the world*
- *countries lose their unique identity*
- *trend towards cultural uniformity*

On the other hand:
- *relationship has never been one-sided*

Global challenges   Is American culture 'American'?   **1**

- *America as a nation of immigrants: ethnic, religious and racial variety*
- *influence of immigrants explains popularity of America's culture*
- *furthermore: a lot of "American" things are not originally American, but European imports: fast food, theme parks etc.*
- *English language as a method of mass communication leads to acceptance of American culture*

Conclusion: *America's influence on a global culture is not "imperialistic" but cosmopolitan.*

Letter:
Dear friends from America and Germany,
The relationship between America and Germany has suffered during the last few years. Different political points of view have led to much discussion. Therefore it is even more important that the younger generation begins to accept the other's culture and way of living. It is the American way of life that is often assumed to be the global lifestyle. People think that American culture has become global. This is not completely wrong. A lot of people like the easy way of living, they respect American self-confidence and love fast food. The Americans, however, take all of this for granted. They often forget that Hollywood, fast food chains and Disneyland are not American inventions, but part of a global development. Americans learned from the Europeans, the Asians and the Africans that came together in the melting pot of the "new world". This should never be forgotten. It is, however, true that the English language plays the most important role in a progress we can no longer stop. Therefore I honestly ask German students to learn the English language properly and American students to remember their European, Asian or African roots and not to think that the American way of life has always played the role it does today. By this we all hope to improve the relationship between the two countries during the coming generations.

Erweiterung   *Paraphrase the difficult words (using the annotations or an English-English dictionary).*

Evaluation   ## 6 [👥] *In groups, discuss the last sentence of the text.*

Verweis auf *Useful phrases* auf Seite 56/57. L: *Present your conclusions.*

Lösungsvorschlag   *On the one hand, America's influence on the world has become obvious. Global American fast food chains, American movies in cinemas all over the world and the dependence of America's economy are only a few examples of worldwide "Americanisation". Though the last few years were not very successful for the popularity of America, the country seems to remain an idol for many countries in the world.*
On the other hand America is a melting pot of many different influences. Its history and culture are a mixture of European and Native American elements, in which European influences dominate life in the big cities. Almost every American family has roots somewhere in Europe. Therefore it is true that America is dependent on the world's different cultures, according to the text "the United States are a replica of the world". Although every country is afraid of American power, it is true that all American traditions originally belong to foreign cultures.

Evaluation   ## 7 *Comment on the argument that ...*

Textproduktion evtl. als schriftliche **Hausaufgabe**.

Lösungsvorschlag   *British culture plays an important role in American lifestyle. The majority of immigrants to America came from England and it is no wonder that the influence of British culture is immense. It is not only the language that led to the close connection between the two countries. It is, however, true that language played an important role in the acceptance of the American way of life. For every student English is compulsory nowadays and nearly every man and woman speaks English anyway. It is not difficult to learn and every part of the entertainment media is based on American originals. In conclusion one can say that the British influence on American culture is*

1 | Global challenges   Is American culture 'American'?

obvious and it can be taken for granted that the teaching of English and American cultures and its effectiveness has opened acceptance for the American lifestyle.

Mind-map   **8 *Revise your mind-map* ...**

Zusatzmaterial   → Klausurvorschlag 1 • Revision files 1 + 2

Lösungsvorschlag   Individuelle Lösungen.

Erweiterung   Zum Abschluss des *Topics* füllen die S die *Revision file 1* (Themenheft, Seite 59) aus. Ein Lösungsvorschlag findet sich hier im Lehrerbuch (Seite 118).

Topic 2: Think globally, eat locally? pp. 18–23

Didaktisches Inhaltsverzeichnis

Bearbeitungszeitraum: 9–11 Unterrichtsstunden

Textsorte/Thema	Unterrichts- methoden	*Input boxes*	Kompetenzen	Textproduktion
Think globally, eat locally?			SB, Seite 18; LB, Seite 30/31	
Combination of visuals/Food from different countries	Partnerarbeit Gruppenarbeit	*Word bank*	Gespräche führen Sehverstehen Bildbeschreibung/ -analyse	*Describing pictures Sharing information Giving a presentation*
Eating with food miles in mind, 2005 (338 words)			SB, Seite 19; LB, Seite 32/33	
Internet news story/Food miles	Kursgespräch Online-Link 4 Zusatzmaterial: Kopiervorlage 3	*Fact file*: Pollution *Useful phrases: Food choices*	Leseverstehen	*Making a comment Writing a formal e-mail*
Organic movement split over air-freighted food, 2007 (592 words)			SB, Seite 20/21; LB, Seite 34–36	
British newspaper article/The organic vs. local debate	Gruppenarbeit Online-Link 5 Zusatzmaterial: Kopiervorlage 4	*Fact file: The Standards Board Useful phrases: Finding pros and cons*	Argumentieren Leseverstehen Gespräche führen	*Finding pros and cons Making a comment Giving an explanation Working with dia- grams (mind-map)*
Organic food's carbon footprint, 2007 (198 words)			SB, Seite 22; LB, Seite 36/37	
Letters to the editor/The organic vs. local debate	Kursgespräch Online-Link 6	*Fact file: Carbon footprints Useful phrases: A letter to the editor*	Recherchieren Leseverstehen Sehverständnis	*Talking about a cartoon Making a summary Writing a formal letter*
[2🎬] We feed the world, 2005 (85 words)			SB, Seite 23; LB, Seite 37–39	
Austrian documentary film/ Mass production of vegetables in greenhouses, industrial food production	*Video transcript* (CD-ROM) Partnerarbeit Online-Link 7 Zusatzmaterial: Klausurvor- schlag 2	*Useful phrases: Talking about documentary style*	Hörverstehen Sehverstehen Mediation	*Making a comment Writing and recording an outline of a conversation on the phone Talking about documentary style Describing and assessing a picture*

2 | Think globally, eat locally? Lead-in: Think globally, eat locally?

Unterrichtsverlauf

Photos | **Lead-in: Think globally, eat locally?** | **p. 18**

HINTERGRUNDINFO

Jamie Oliver, the English celebrity chef, was born in Essex in 1975 and is popular for his fresh and organic food. He started his career as a chef in 1998 with the cooking programme "The Naked Chef", which is still his nickname. Since then he has had several additional TV series and written ten books. Oliver is also the public face of the British supermarket chain "Sainsbury's" but is also known

for his charity work for which he was appointed MBE (Member of the Order of the British Empire) by the Queen. There are several of his "Fifteen" charity restaurants worldwide in which disadvantaged teenagers can work and are trained in the hospitality sector.

***Quotations:** Based on article "How the world eats" by Brian Walsh, in: Time, 25/6/07–2/7/07.*

Discussion
Die S nehmen die Fotos und Zitate in einer Stillarbeitsphase zur Kenntnis, anschließend Kursgespräch mit kurzer Bildbeschreibung. L gibt einige Gesprächsimpulse:
Have you eaten any of these dishes?
If you want to go to a restaurant in Germany, what choice do you have?
Why do or don't you agree with Jamie Oliver's preference for locally-grown food?
Looking at the quotations: Do they contradict or suppport each other?

Discussion | **1 *Support the above statements ...***

Lösungsvorschlag | ***Food and society***
- *Religious taboos*
  Muslims don't eat pork, don't drink alcohol, don't eat or drink anything from sunrise to sunset during Ramadan. Jews only eat kosher food.
- *Class structure*
  Rich people go to restaurants rather than eat at home. Poorer people tend to have more fast food, sweet or fat snacks. In some countries people live on what others have thrown away. As food gets more and more expensive, people can afford less. What we know about food (education) also plays a role.
- *Geography*
  A lot of countries are responsible for the availability of certain food. The kind of food depends on the climate. The geography (climate) is responsible for the availability of certain foods.
- *Economy*
  What and how we eat depends on the amount of money you can spend (cf. class structure) as well as the "time-is-money aspect". In many families there's no time to cook traditional meals. They rely on convenience or fast food.

Erweiterung
Vorbereitung einer kurzen Präsentation über Essen bzw. die Essgewohnheiten in einem beliebigen Land.

Discussion | **2 [👥] *What is your favourite food?***

Die S tauschen sich über ihr Lieblingsessen aus. L stellt bei Bedarf einige Wendungen zur Verfügung, z. B. *to catch fish, to prepare food, to slaughter animals, to cook dinner and meals, to change eating habits, to grow fruit and vegetables, to go on a diet, to fight obesity.*

Alternative
Möglichkeit zur Partnersuche unabhängig von der Sitzordnung: Die Wortgruppen werden aufgelöst und getrennt auf Kärtchen geschrieben (z. B. *to catch, fish, to prepare, food, to slaughter, animals, etc.*) und durchgemischt. Die S ziehen Kärtchen und finden sich in Paaren zusammen.

Think globally, eat locally? **Lead-in: Think globally, eat locally?** | **2**

Discussion **3 Which countries do you associate with the following foods: ...**

Die S beschäftigen sich mit den typischen Essgewohnheiten anderer Länder.

Lösungsvorschlag
- *tandoori – India*
- *fish & chips – England*
- *cheese – Switzerland*
- *hamburger – USA*
- *sushi – Japan*
- *bratwurst – Germany*
- *pizza – Italy*
- *sweet and sour pork – China*
- *döner kebap – Turkey*
- *paella – Spain*

The associations might be positive (tasty – Indian food; cheap – pizza; healthy – sushi, paella; quick – bratwurst) or negative (expensive – fish & chips, Swiss cheese; unhealthy/ fat – hamburger, döner kebab, bratwurst; hot – Indian food).

All of these foods represent different countries. As they are a typical part of individual traditions these associations should be regarded as positive. Although fish and chips or hamburgers might not be seen as a delicious meal, they are part of American and British lifestyles. People all over the world enjoy foreign meals and the foods mentioned are specialities a lot of people like. It should, however, be regarded critically that sushi loses its individuality by worldwide "Running Sushi" companies. Chinese restaurants are opening on every corner and you can order a pizza wherever you want. The foods are globalised and will soon lose the associations to their home countries.

Erweiterung Die S überlegen weitere landestypische Gerichte, z. B. *pelmeni – Russia, tacos – Mexico, gulash – Hungary, etc.*

Sharing information **4 [👥] How many meals do you have each day?**

Verweis auf die *Word bank words*. Die S tauschen sich in Kleingruppen über individuelle Essgewohnheiten aus.

Presentation **5 [👥] In small groups analyse eating habits ...**

Die S analysieren deutsche Essgewohnheiten und reflektieren dabei ihr eigenes Essverhalten. Anschließend präsentieren sie die Gruppenarbeitsergebnisse im Plenum.

Lösungsvorschlag *Aspects mentioned could include:*
- *less time to prepare meals or to eat them at set times,*
- *economy moves on, time is money, shorter lunch breaks and longer working hours,*
- *"culinary destiny" – what grows where, price of certain food,*
- *influence of food advertisement ("I love it"), cooking shows,*
- *mothers aren't at home to cook time-consuming meals because they have full-time jobs.*

Erweiterung L stellt folgende **Hausaufgabe**: *Study the choice of cooking shows on TV and discuss the following statement: "Star cooks are the new celebrities."* Die S werden der Aussage wahrscheinlich zustimmen und Jamie Oliver (siehe **Hintergrundinfo**, S. 30) oder Tim Mälzer erwähnen.

2   Think globally, eat locally?   Eating with food miles in mind

Internet text | **Eating with food miles in mind** | **p. 19**

HINTERGRUNDINFO

The term **food miles** was first used by Tim Lang, professor at the City University of London. The idea was to create a simple system to show the often hidden ecologic, social and economic consequences of food production. In October 2007 the EU parliament decided to agree on importing organic food by plane if it is obvious that farmers in developing countries profit from it. This was a compromise between those who support the concept of food miles and others claiming that the social aspect of it needs to be strengthened by also looking at so-called "fair miles".

The **LifeCycles Project Society** is a non-profit and community-based organisation in the Greater Victoria community in British Columbia/Canada and is mainly run by young people. Its aims are to evoke and strengthen the awareness of food, health and urban sustainability. To this purpose the members initiate and support projects in the Victorian area. The Society started in 1994 and was the result of an international youth exchange with Santiago/Chile. The focus was on the home environment and the examination of the quality of urban community life. The Society's first and main initiatives include tackling the shortage of community gardens, the creation of model gardens to show organic methods of cultivation, a program called "Sharing backyard program" where people who have a garden share it with people who don't own any land to do gardening, and the arrangement of conferences and workshops for young people to make them aware of food issues. The Project's maxim is: "Think globally, act locally".

Lernwortschatz   locally farmed, food miles, to be of increasing concern, to go global, a growing source of …, sustainability, carbon dioxide (CO_2), to contribute to the atmosphere, greenhouse gases, to cut emissions, producer, consumer, exhaust gases, herbicides, pesticides, fertilizer, recyclable, biodegradable

Materialien   → Online-Link: 601002-0004

Discussion   L fordert die S auf, die Textinhalte kurz auf Deutsch zusammenzufassen: *Summarise the text in German.* Weitere L-Impulse: *Have you ever heard of food miles? Do you have an idea what food miles are? In which respect are they relevant to the process of global warming?* Die S werden vermutlich feststellen, dass sie sich bisher nur wenige Gedanken über die Transportwege gemacht haben, die viele Nahrungsmittel zurücklegen. L: *How do you feel about food miles now? Surprised, astonished, shocked?*

Comprehension   **1 *Look at the following phrases and comment …***

Lösungsvorschlag   **a)** *Metaphorical expressions/alliteration (agreeable sound, hammering-in effect, create a picture in the reader's mind, add vitality to the text).*
b) *From the text: food miles/mileage (l. 5, l. 25), the larger the load (l. 26).*
Other similar phrases: from the cradle to the grave, from here to eternity, from top to toe, from morning to night, from here to there, from Monday to Friday, from nine to five, etc.

Analysis   **2 *Analyse how the author uses specific examples***

Die S befassen sich mit dem Text im Detail und analysieren weitere Beispiele. Verweis auf *Fact file* zu *Pollution*.

Lösungsvorschlag   *Contrast: Locally farmed chicken (Canada) vs. New Zealand venison. Four to ten times as much as if bought locally. Lamb chops from Australia, tuna steaks from Hawaii.*
Exotic: Chinese pine nuts, snow peas from Kenya. Peruvian asparagus, Pakistani mangoes.
Effect: *Create a notion of the long distances and the amount of (unnecessary) pollution.*

The author uses examples of common foods that travel a lot of miles. These foods are among those whose trip mostly goes all around the world. It could therefore cause the readers to reflect on especially these foods, for example, meat and fish more carefully. Examples like fruits and

32

Think globally, eat locally? Eating with food miles in mind | **2**

vegetables from Italy or Spain would not have the same effect as the steaks mentioned from New Zealand or Australia. Foods that are transported by plane show the amount of carbon dioxide better that those that go by truck. Therefore they are used to support the author's hope to attract the reader's attention.

Erweiterung L: *Find the places mentioned on the map at the end of your textbook.*

Discussion ### 3 Calculate the food miles for a meal you eat today

Die S berechnen die *food miles* ihrer eigenen Mahlzeiten und beurteilen sie. L: *Comment on your findings. Did you expect them? Will you change your behaviour towards food?*

Lösungsvorschlag a) Individuelle S-Antworten.
b) *Other aspects measured in "… miles": the miles I walk per day, the miles my e-mails travel within a few seconds, the miles my clothes have been transported from their origin to the shop, the miles my money goes after I have spent it, etc.*

Text production ### 4 Creative writing

Zusatzmaterial → Kopiervorlage 3 (Global food – word power)

Verweis auf *Useful phrases* zu *Food choices*. Die S schreiben die E-Mail als **Hausaufgabe**, einige Beispiele werden im Plenum vorgelesen.

Lösungsvorschlag *Dear Ms Durgahee,*
I read your article on food miles and I think it is very interesting. However, it would be very difficult for me to rely only on locally produced, seasonal food as you suggest at the end of your article. By chance I talked with my grandmother about it. She told me that food has traditionally been seasonal. They had apples, cabbage and canned fruit and vegetables in winter and fresh tomatoes, peas, lettuce and fresh fruit in summer. Well, I don't need strawberries at Christmas, but oranges, for example, have become very common in winter for me. I need the vitamins, don't I? Apart from that, I don't know whether other healthy products could be produced in Germany to meet the demand. I'm thinking of beef (which in our household comes from Argentina) or fish and prawns. And a life without chocolate would be very boring. But most of all I would miss certain drinks such as cola, coffee or tea. My friends and I like to have a fruit cocktail or smoothie after school. They are mostly based on bananas, pineapples and coconuts and, as you know, they don't grow here. If I had to do without all those things, it would certainly reduce the quality of my life and that's not what I want.
Best wishes,

Dear Mr Quest,
I really enjoyed reading your article about the miles our daily foods travel and I really started to think about it while shopping. For half a year I've now been trying to buy and eat only products from my region. In that year I have spent more money on food than before. Most of the local products are more expensive than imports from far away. Furthermore a lot of food like vegetables and fruit and even fish are quite hard to get without buying imports from southern countries. They are, however, necessary for a balanced diet. It is true that one can do without some imported food, others, however, are quite important. I therefore still think your documentation on CNN was very informative, however, a bit one-sided. Problems of subsisting without imported foods should be mentioned, too.
Sincerely yours,

Erweiterung Zum Abschluss dieses Abschnitts kann **Kopiervorlage 3** (Seite 95) eingesetzt werden. Das Arbeitsblatt fast den themenspezifischen Wortschatz zusammen und festigt die Lexik.

2 | Think globally, eat locally? Organic movement split over air-freighted food

Newspaper article | **Organic movement split over air-freighted food** | pp. 20/21

HINTERGRUNDINFO

The **FairTrade Foundation** is an independent and non-profit organisation and is part of a network of organisations, including FairTrade International. Its aim is to establish justice and sustainable development as a basis for trade structures and practices so that every individual can live in dignity. In order to achieve that, the organisation maintains trade partnerships and demonstrates alternatives. The key areas are the licensing of the FairTrade mark, working with partners to support producer organisations and their networks and giving information to the public to raise awareness of the need for FairTrade and the FairTrade mark.

The **Soil Association**, which is now the UK's leading organic organisation, was founded in 1946 by a group of farmers, scientists and nutritionists. As it is not an association supported by the government, the charity relies on donations, memberships and the public to carry out its work. With over 180 staff working both in the Bristol headquarters, regional centres and as certification inspectors across the country, the Soil Association is UK's leading

campaigning and certification organisation for organic food and farming. Its symbol is the UK's most well-known trademark for organic produce and is found on more than 70 per cent of all UK organic products.

Blue Skies is a company importing fresh fruit from Egypt, South Africa, Ghana and Brazil and was founded in 1998. In order to keep the fruit as fresh as possible the products are cut and packed where they grow and delivered within two days. Blue Skies employs more than 2,000 people, works with the Soil Association and Fair Trade, and also runs different environmental projects like land and forest conservation, re-forestation and composting.

Riverford Farm is a cooperation of 13 family run farms in South Devon, which gives them the opportunity to grow more than 85 different vegetables. The company is one of the largest organic vegetable home delivery box schemes in the UK. Guy Watson started farming in 1985 and achieved complete organic status in 1987.

Lernwortschatz organic, to air-freight, ethical dilemma, to be preferable to sth else, a booming movement, prosperity, integrity, climate change, flown-in food, environmental standards, conventional local food, to generate CO_2, self-imposed ban, to take priority, substantial, carbon footprint, to maintain the status quo, credibility, to offset flights, sustainable, to evolve

Materialien → Online-Link: 601002-0005

Discussion | **1 Explain the difference ...**

Die S erklären den Unterschied zwischen den Begriffen *locally grown* und *organic* im Kursgespräch. L: *What food should we buy – locally grown or organic?* Antwort: *Both locally grown and organic is the ideal solution that is seldom found.* Die S knüpfen einen Bezug zu ihrem Alltag und stellen fest, dass es nicht einfach ist, die in **b)** geforderten Nahrungsmittel zu finden. L: *If you didn't find any in your grocery store, where else could you look for them?* Antwort: *In an organic food store.*

Lösungsvorschlag **a)** *Locally grown means from the area where the product (fruit, vegetable, meat, eggs, etc.) is grown or produced. Organic means without the use of pesticides or other chemicals.*
b) Individuelle S-Ergebnisse.

Discussion | **2 How exactly do our choices of food purchases ...**

Möglicherweise zeitaufwändige, aber äußerst interessante Diskussion. L: *Try to explain the relationship between organic, non-organic, local and not local with the help of the arrows.* Die Aufgabe bezieht den Text bereits mit ein.

Lösungsvorschlag • *Trend towards organic because products are not treated with chemicals, animals are "happy", not from industrial sized farms.*

34

Think globally, eat locally? Organic movement split over air-freighted food | 2

- *But organic products might come to us from the other end of the world and thus might have lost taste, vitamins.*
- *If they are not local (bananas, oranges) they might have been treated in order to stay fresh and they have been transported over long distances and have caused a lot of pollution, i.e. they might be healthy for us but not for the planet.*
- *Local products, in contrast, may be treated with chemicals (for example because the climate forces the farmers to) but they have been transported over short distances and are thus fresh and retain their vitamins.*

Erweiterung   L: *Where would the category "seasonal" go?* Mögliche Antwort: *"Seasonal" would be close to local but restricts the choice of fruit and vegetable enormously.*

Discussion   **3 Discuss possible reasons ...**

Die S setzen sich mit dem Hintergrund der Ergebnisse, die die *Soil Association* bei einer Umfrage herausgefunden hat, auseinander.

Lösungsvorschlag   *Conventional local food has always been there. It is known, you know what you get and you know how to prepare it. It doesn't spoil so fast. It's cheaper than imported food and we want to support the local farmer.*

Comprehension   **4 Describe and comment on the dilemma ...**

Die S erstellen (ggf. in Partnerarbeit) eine Tabelle, in der die Argumente gegenübergestellt werden. Anschließend erfolgt eine Präsentation der Ergebnisse mit Hilfe einer Folie.

Lösungsvorschlag

organic	*fair trade*
local (English)	*imports*
strict environmental standards	*development of the Third World*
farmers can't grow enough	*1/3 organic products imported*
conventional	*organic import*
ban air-freighted food	*help far-away producers (who have a small carbon footprint)*

Discussion   **5 What is more important ...**

Die S setzten sich im Kursgespräch mit der Produktion und Lieferung von Nahrungsmitteln auseinander.

Lösungsvorschlag   *Food and vegetables that are shipped over long distances ripen on the way and not under the sun, and thus have no vitamins. Reflecting on the taste it might be quite important how food is shipped and handled, but also how it is grown. A lot of vegetables become inedible, if they are treated badly during their journey from southern countries. Furthermore the more organic they were grown, the better they taste. Tomatoes from greenhouses in the Netherlands for example taste worse than local tomatoes from organic plantations. They are, however, much cheaper than the local ones. Therefore the price depends again on how food is grown. Organic food that has been transported in good conditions will taste quite good but also be more expensive. Summing up one can say that the better food tastes the more it costs.*

	How food is grown	*How food is shipped and handled*
Taste	*Positive influence: natural farming techniques in the sun, home-grown and fresh.* *Negative: mass production in greenhouses.*	*Negative: ripen in a refrigerated shipping container – taste suffers; without the sun crops might taste watery, not like the "real" ones.*

2 | Think globally, eat locally? Organic food's carbon footprint

Price	Cheap: industrialised/conventional production of produce. Expensive: organic, local (sometimes).	Increases with distance, cost in oil usage.
Healthiness	Positive: organic, full of vitamins. Negative: non-organic, use of pesticides, synthetic fertilizers, industrialised production – lower nutrition values.	Negative: when shipped over long distances – fewer vitamins. Positive: distance between grower and point of sale/consumer short – freshness.

Discussion

6 [⚏] *Finding pros and cons: …*

Zusatzmaterial

→ **Kopiervorlage 4 (The global food system)**

Verweis auf *Useful phrases* zu *Finding pros and cons* (S. 21) und *Useful phrases* auf S. 55/56 sowie auf *Fact file: The Standards Board* (S. 21). In Gruppen von je sechs S werden die Argumente gesammelt. Das *Role play: Anna Bradley as chairwoman as she decides on the compromise* wird entweder parallel erarbeitet oder zu Hause vorbereitet und später im Plenum vorgespielt. Die Zusammenfassung der Ergebnisse kann als schriftliche Textproduktion in Form einer Erörterung oder eines Dialogs erfolgen:

1. *Is it acceptable to air-freight organic food? Consider that the prosperity of African farmers depends on the answer as well as the health of our planet.*
2. *Write and act out a dialogue between a local farmer and a shopper about the organic-vs.-local debate at the weekly market. Use the arguments above.*

Erweiterung

Zum Abschluss dieses Abschnitts kann **Kopiervorlage 4** (Seite 96) eingesetzt werden. Die S entwickeln ein *leaflet* zum Thema *The global food system* und gestalten das Layout am Computer.

Letters to the editor

Organic food's carbon footprint   p. 22

Lernwortschatz

carbon footprint, primary footprint, secondary footprint, emission, carbon dioxide (CO_2), greenhouse gases, organic, organic certification, to turn consumers off, withdrawal, air-freighted produce, developing countries, to rely on, environmental impact, greenhouse, aviation industry, environmentalist, climate change

Discussion

Als Hinführung dient ein Kursgespräch. L-Impulse: *Have a look at and comment on the cartoon. Study the Fact file and comment on the metaphorical meaning of the term.*
Name some of the arguments from the role play again that the Kenyan farmer and Anna Bradley have used as for air-freighted organic produce.

Lösungsvorschlag

Idea that you should do sth good for the environment when you have "committed an environmental sin". Size of footprint, leave your footprint, can be traced (in forensics), should be reduced.

Comprehension

1 *In just two sentences each, summarise the standpoints …*

L: *What newspapers are the letters taken from? What does that mean for the credibility of the contents?* Mögliche Antwort: *"The Times" is a broadsheet, reliable information, appeals to educated, interested readers (proven after having looked at the two letter writers).*

Erweiterung

Vorab evtl. Einzelpräsentation: *Survey British newspapers.*

Lösungsvorschlag

- *Nearly a million African farmers would lose their income if the organic certification was taken away from their products. Their carbon footprint is smaller as they do not use that much energy.*
- *The Soil Association discusses air-freight as aviation is growing and air-freight is an essential part of it.*

Think globally, eat locally? We feed the world | 2

Research

2 Find information about the work of the ...

Kann auch als vorbereitende **Hausaufgabe** für die Stunde gestellt werden.

Lösungsvorschlag siehe **Hintergrundinfo** zu *Soil Association*, S. 34.

Evaluation

3 How can you reduce your carbon footprint?

Zu Aufgabe **a)** kann in Einzelarbeit eine Präsentation erstellt werden. L: *Prepare a short presentation of your suggestions. Include your opinion about the effect with others and accept the reactions from the course.*

Lösungsvorschlag
a) *Reduce central heating, recycle, separate waste, reduce amount of water used by taking shorter showers, use public transport or the bicycle instead of car, turn off mobile phone charger, light, etc., buy local food, watch less TV, turn off the standby, note how your food is packed, etc.*
b) *All of these suggestions are definitely good ideas to reduce wasting energy in private households. Therefore I'm sure that these points would work for many other people I know. They are all part of our daily routine and easy to recognise and carry out. All of these measures could help to reduce the environmental pollution without any difficulties.*

Text production

4 Write a letter to the editor about reducing carbon footprints

Verweis auf *Useful phrases* zu *A letter to the editor.* L: *Before you start, decide what you want to focus on in your letter.*

Lösungsvorschlag
Dear Sir or Madam,
It is true that the carbon footprints which are produced by the transportation of food in planes are enormous. We should, however, begin to reduce the environmental pollution in our surroundings before we start to discuss the transport of fruit and vegetables from East African countries. It is always easy to point at others while we are all driving around in cars or going on holiday by plane. In my opinion flights in order to transport food are more necessary and important to our living standard than all the holiday planes. It is not our job to criticise poor African farmers but to start reducing the waste of energy in our own households.
Sincerely yours,

Video clip

[2🎞] We feed the world — p. 23

HINTERGRUNDINFO

Website of the film on mass production of vegetables in greenhouses, industrial food production: http://www.we-feed-the-world.at/

Erwin Wagenhöfer (born 1961): Austrian freelance writer and filmmaker.

Jean Ziegler (born 1934): UN Special Rapporteur on "The Right to Nutrition" and senior professor of sociology at the University of Geneva and Sorbonne, Paris.

"We feed the world" is a documentary about food and globalisation. In his film, Erwin Wagenhöfer follows food around the globe, thus giving insights into the production of what we eat. An interview with Jean Ziegler, who currently holds the office of

UN Rapporteur for the Committee on "The right to Nutrition", functions as a frame, but fishermen, farmers, and biologists are also given a voice. Besides, Peter Brabeck, concern director of Nestlé International, which is the biggest food producing company worldwide, is also asked to comment on the topic. In Austria the film has been the most successful documentary ever. In German-speaking countries about 600,000 people went to see it.

A book with the same title (**"We feed the world"**) by Erwin Wagenhöfer and Max Annas has been published (Orange Press) and gives background information as well as further examples regarding the topics of the film.

2 | Think globally, eat locally? We feed the world

Lernwortschatz *greenhouse, irrigation, crop, soil, transportation costs, retail price, agricultural market, conveyor belt, packaging, subsidy, enlightening, gloomy*

Materialien → Film, Track 2

Text production

1 Mediation

[2🎬] Die S müssen vor der Bearbeitung von Aufgabe 1 **Track 2** auf der CD-ROM gesehen haben. Das kann entweder gemeinsam im Medienraum oder als **Hausaufgabe** geschehen. Verweis auf *Useful phrases* zu *Talking about documentary style*. Nach **a)** erfolgt kurze mündliche Zusammenfassung als Kursgespräch: *What did you find interesting/new/surprising?* Die schriftliche *summary* kann als **Hausaufgabe** erfolgen.

Lösungsvorschlag
a) *Almeria, southern Spain; 1960s water pipelines, irrigation installed; growing tomatoes on substrate (rock wool); 3,000 hours of sunshine a year; economic boom after building of greenhouses; population growth from 1,000 to 100,000; markets in southern hemisphere destroyed, farmers have to emigrate; African workers in greenhouses, live there, trucks with tomatoes drive 3,000 km through Europe*
b) *In the beginning the film explains how the area of Almeria became so important in the production of vegetables. The Spanish government supported the area with water and settled the farmers there. Moreover, it shows how the plants are fed and how the water is recycled. All of this changed the area of Almeria from a poor stretch of countryside to a wealthy area. Small villages became towns and everyone got wealthier. This development of growing plants in greenhouses means that no farmer in Africa has any chance of selling his products. Although the market is getting more difficult Spanish greenhouse products are sold more easily than African products. The farmers there have to emigrate as they can't survive from their work.*

Comprehension

2 Second viewing

Verweis auf Vokabelliste *(add to your notes according to the tasks)* und auf *Useful phrases* zu *Talking about documentary style*. Die S beantworten die Fragen zum Textverständnis in Einzel- oder Partnerarbeit und beziehen sich dabei auch auf die Bilder. Ggf. erfolgt die schriftliche Beantwortung der Fragen zusätzlich als schriftliche **Hausaufgabe**.

Lösungsvorschlag
1. *Main producer of vegetable in winter; farmers from the hills came down to work here but golden years are over, 10–15 years ago good wages, competition with countries with similar climate.*
2. *Dumping; European vegetables offered for 1/3 of the local prices; destruction of African markets.*
3. *EU, USA subsidise their farmers with 349 billion dollar a year (more than 1 billion dollar a day); destruction of agriculture in southern hemisphere where there are mainly small-scale farms; farmers have no choice – have to emigrate.*
4. *Hardly any commentary; only pictures and explanation of Lieven Bruneel; written commentary as introduction and at the end; dispassionate; enlightening but gloomy; commentary by Jean Ziegler.*
5. *Not overly didactic; makers just try to make their point; effect of lacking comment of film-makers stronger than with it, shocking effect of plain/bleak facts but: demonstrative style would influence the viewer more, perhaps even manipulate; discussion about what arouses more emotions.*

Evaluation

3 Comment on ...

Die S befassen sich mit dem Kommentar von Erwin Wagenhöfer in einem Kursgespräch und nehmen dazu Stellung.

Think globally, eat locally? We feed the world | 2

Lösungsvorschlag *Erwin Wagenhöfer wants us to think about where our food comes from and how it is produced. Food is close to everyone. So we should be more aware of that and get informed, for example about the European Union's food regulations. We could join the Slow Food Organisation or buy Fair Trade products. The question is whether consumers can have an influence on the production of food. We could support local farmers by buying locally produced food or study the labels of supermarket fruit and vegetables and inform ourselves about the place of production. Wagenhöfer has shown that we in the industrialised world waste food while so many are starving elsewhere. We really shouldn't waste bread or water any longer. The comments by Jean Ziegler are real eye-openers and encourage us to change the system of "feeding the world". Genetically manipulated food and bio-fuel are only some of the problems we should think about and deal with.*

Erweiterung L: *Does this documentary confirm/challenge any prejudices? Does it make you change anything?*

Writing an outline **4 [👥] *Work in pairs. Imagine a telephone call ...***

Es folgt die Ausarbeitung des imaginären Telefongesprächs zwischen L. Bruneel und J. Ziegler unter Einbeziehung der vorangegangenen Arbeitsergebnisse. L erteilt Zusatzauftrag an interessierten S: *Do some research on Jean Ziegler and his work.*

Zusatzmaterial → Klausurvorschlag 2 • Revision file 3

Erweiterung Zum Abschluss des *Topics* füllen die S den ersten Teil von *Revision file* 3 (Themenheft, Seite 61) aus. Nach der Bearbeitung von *Topic* 3 wird die *Revision file* komplettiert. Ein Lösungsvorschlag findet sich hier im Lehrerbuch (Seite 119).

39

3 | Saving the planet   Didaktisches Inhaltsverzeichnis

Topic 3: Saving the planet

pp. 24–33

Didaktisches Inhaltsverzeichnis

Bearbeitungszeitraum: 12–14 Unterrichtsstunden

Textsorte/Thema	Unterrichts- methoden	Input boxes	Kompetenzen	Textproduktion
Saving the planet (166 words)			SB, Seite 24; LB, Seite 42/43	
Combination of visuals and quotations/ Industry and nature	Kursgespräch Zusatzmaterial: Kopiervorlage 5	*Word bank: Renewable energy*	Sehverstehen Leseverstehen Gespräche führen Bildbeschreibung/ -analyse	*Describing and assessing pictures Writing a personal letter Making a comment Giving an explanation*
'Credit cards' to ration individuals' carbon, 2006 (310 words)			SB, Seite 25; LB, Seite 43–45	
British newspaper article/Carbon use of individuals		*Tip: Writing a story*	Recherchieren Leseverstehen	*Writing a formal letter Writing a science fiction story Making a comment*
Red alert! Climate change takes its toll on Scotland, 2006 (518 words)			SB, Seite 26/27; LB, Seite 45–47	
British newspaper article/Scotland as example of the effects of climate change	Gruppenarbeit Online-Link 8	*Fact files: Scotland/ Global warming Useful phrases: Talking about credibility*	Recherchieren Leseverstehen Gespräche führen Argumentieren	*Giving an explanation Giving a report*
Global warming profits, 2007 (270 words)			SB, Seite 28; LB, Seite 47–49	
Canadian newspaper article/ Al Gore	Online-Link 9	*Useful phrases: Discussion the tone*	Leseverstehen Statistiken analysieren	*Working with diagrams Making a comment Talking about tone and register*
Eine unbequeme Wahrheit, 2006 (346 words)			SB, Seite 29; LB, Seite 49–51	
German magazine article/Al Gore's documentary „An Inconvenient Truth"	Online-Link 10	*VIP file: Al Gore*	Leseverstehen Mediation	*Writing a film review Talking about a cartoon*
A friend of the earth, 2000 (800 words)			SB, Seite 30/31; LB, Seite 51–53	
Novel excerpt/ Fiction by T.C. Boyle	Gruppenarbeit Online-Link 11 Zusatzmaterial: Kopiervorlage 6	*VIP file: T.C. Boyle Useful phrases: Talking about short films*	Leseverstehen Hörverstehen Sehverstehen Mediation Gespräche führen Recherchieren Argumentieren	*Writing a text focusing on tone Making a comment Making a summary Writing a letter*

Saving the planet Didaktisches Inhaltsverzeichnis **3**

Textsorte/Thema	Unterrichts-methoden	*Input boxes*	Kompetenzen	Textproduktion
[5 ◉] Severn Suzuki speaks in Rio, 2006 (904 words)			SB, Seite 32; LB, Seite 54/55	
Speech/America's global policy options	Tapescript (CD-ROM) Partnerarbeit Rollenspiel Online-Link 12	*VIP file: Severn Suzuki* *Useful phrases:* *Rhetorical devices*	Hörverstehen Recherchieren Gespräche führen Leseverstehen	*Working with rhetorical devices*
Let's not worry about climate change! (268 words)			SB, Seite 33; LB, Seite 55–57	
Advertisement/ Sarcastic view of aviation	Gruppenarbeit Online-Link 13 Zusatzmaterial: Klausurvor-schlag 3	*Useful phrases:* *Describing graphic elements*	Leseverstehen Hörverstehen Sehverstehen Gespräche führen Recherchieren Argumentieren	*Giving a PowerPoint presentation* *Making a comment* *Describing a picture* *Talking about tone and register*

3 Saving the planet   Lead-in: Saving the planet

Unterrichtsverlauf

Photos | **Lead-in: Saving the planet** | p. 24

HINTERGRUNDINFO

Charles Robert Redford (born 18/8/1936 in Santa Monica, California) is an Academy-Award-winning American actor ("Out of Africa", "The Horse Whisperer"), film director, producer and environmentalist. He is the founder of the "Sundance Film Festival" for independent film (in 1981, non-profit), the "Sundance Channel" (eco-themed television programming) and "The Green", a block of environmental programming launched in April, 2007. Redford is a forceful advocate for the "Clean Air Act" and the "Energy Conservation and Protection Act", and has testified on Capitol Hill. He organised the 1989 "Sundance Global Warming Conference" and bridges popular culture and art, politics and movie stardom, environmentalism and entertainment. Redford supports "Youth Speaks" (non-profit organisation that presents spoken-word performances): "Words are just words without action. But I think what we're seeing here today with these poets is the beginning of action."

University of the Witwatersrand (Johannesburg): Its origins lie in the "South African School of Mines", established in Kimberly in 1896. Witwatersrand University was granted full university status in 1922 and is a leading South African university situated in Johannesburg. Wits' mission statement: "Changing Your Future by Challenging Your Mind". Witwatersrand University has produced four Nobel Prize laureates: Nelson Mandela (Peace), Aaron Klug (Chemistry), Sydney Bremer (Medicine), Nadine Gordimer (Literature). More than 20 Wits alumni (Witsies) have been knighted in the UK. At the 78th Academy Awards held in Los Angeles in 2006, six Witsies walked away with an Oscar for the film "Tsotsi". Wits is home to one of the largest fossil collections in the Southern hemisphere, boasts 14 museums and two art galleries. Wits University has got about 25,000 students (2006).

Discussion Kursgespräch: Robert Redford's role as an environmentalist. What aspects of the (dangers for the) environment are presented in the pictures?

Discussion | **1 Wind power is not the only way …**

Die Aufgabe kann als vorbereitende **Hausaufgabe** gestellt werden. Es folgt eine Einzelpräsentation im Plenum. Alternativ ist die Bearbeitung auch in Partner-/Gruppenarbeit denkbar.

Lösungsvorschlag
- Wind power (wind flowing over the blades make the blades turn, they are connected to a shaft that turns a generator that produces electricity).
- Solar power (converting sunlight into energy, photovoltaic – conversion of sunlight into electricity using a photovoltaic cell or solar cell; solar thermal – sun heats up water stored in a dark vessel, used to generate steam, which powers a turbine).
- Hydropower (moving water that flows or falls, tidal movement of oceans).
- Geothermal power (heat from inside the earth).

Erweiterung L: Find out about the world's largest wind farm, the "Horse Hollow Wind Energy Centre" in Texas.

Text production | **2 After reading the quotations, …**

Zusatzmaterial → Kopiervorlage 5 (Climate change made easy)

Lösungsvorschlag a) Statement 1: Protecting the environment as a matter of national defence.
Statement 2: Environmental issues are not as pressing as other issues.
Statement 3: Individuals think they can't do much.
Statement 4: Providing food is more important than protecting the environment.

b) Individuelle S-Antworten.
c) *Statement 3:* Dear Mr Fang Jie,
It might be true that it would not change anything if you decided not to drive or if you turned off your lights. The problem is, however, that if everybody thought like you nobody would recycle or separate waste, everybody would leave his lights on, his TV in the standby modus and go everywhere by car. In every single case it would not harm our environment much, but all together a lack of environmental consciousness would be a disaster to our world. Therefore it would be better to motivate friends, colleagues and others to reduce the private waste of energy and emission of carbon dioxide than to react in a frustrated way and think that an individual could not change anything. From now on we have to all work together, as environmental pollution is increasing in an alarming way.
Sincerely yours,

Erweiterung Zum Abschluss dieses Abschnitts kann **Kopiervorlage 5** (Seite 97) eingesetzt werden. Das Arbeitsblatt enthält eine Grafik zum Thema Klimawandel. Die S tauschen sich in Partnerarbeit über die dargestellten Entwicklungen aus.

Newspaper article **'Credit cards' to ration individuals' carbon use** p. 25

HINTERGRUNDINFO

David Miliband (born 1965) is a member of the Labour Party and a Member of Parliament. Since June 2007 he has been holding the post of the UK's Foreign Secretary.

Credit card-style trading system: Some information about how the system, introduced by environment secretary David Miliband, would work if established in the UK: The system is based on a nationwide carbon rationing scheme, which could come into operation within five years, giving everybody an amount of carbon they could expend on a range of products (e.g. food, energy and travel). Every time a citizen buys a product, a personal "credit card", on which one's individual amount of carbon is recorded, is swiped. The possibility to trade with carbon one does not need or purchasing more carbon for one's own use is part of the idea. However, there are still questions to be solved like the risk of fraud, the relationship to ID cards, and, of course, costs. David Miliband is convinced that the suggestion is important and necessary in order to fight global warming and should be introduced as soon as possible.

Lernwortschatz *emission, trading scheme, to impose, global warming, carbon rations, the public sector, proposal, measure, open market, to shift, consumer, fuel*

Research **1 [💻] Before you read the text, consult the Internet …**

Lösungsvorschlag The emission trading scheme for businesses is one of the most important points in climate policy. The European Union Emission Trading Scheme (EU ETS) is the largest multinational greenhouse gas emissions trading scheme in the world. With the emission trading schemes as one of the ways to try to fulfil the aims of the Kyoto protocol big companies have to monitor their carbon emissions. Every year they have to reduce their carbon emissions by a certain amount and report these numbers to the European Union.

Comprehension **2 List Mr Miliband's suggestions …**

Kursgespräch: *How would you reduce the emission of carbon?* Die S sammeln Ideen und vergleichen sie mit Milibands Vorschlägen: *What do you think of Miliband's ideas?*

Lösungsvorschlag
- limit on the carbon each person produces
- credit card-style trading system
- pay for air travel, electricity, gas, petrol with carbon rations/carbon points and cash

43

3 | Saving the planet 'Credit cards' to ration individuals' carbon use

- expansion of emissions trading system for business, public sector and similar system for individuals
- citizens get personal carbon allowance
- people who cut pollution can sell their surplus
- people who continue to produce pollution must buy credits on the open market
- ban products such as inefficient light bulbs, devices that waste power while on standby
- new environmental taxes
- shift the cost of pollution onto consumers
- consumers must make automatic payments

Discussion

3 Why is there so much talk about carbon ...

Diese Aufgabe bietet sich zur interdisziplinären Behandlung mit naturwissenschaftlichen Fächern *(physics, chemistry, biology)* an.

Lösungsvorschlag

A high emission of carbon into the atmosphere leads to an extension of the hole in the ozone layer. As a result the sun can warm up the earth without us being protected by the ozone layer and the whole world is getting warmer, the eternal ice at the North Pole has begun to melt, the sea level is rising and environmental catastrophes like tornados or tsunamis have become more regular. This development has become well known by the term "greenhouse effect" and is the reason why carbon is the gas that is mostly talked about in this connection. Another element that is very dangerous is uranium. We all know uranium arms, uranium power stations and the catastrophes it can cause. A small leak in a uranium power station can destroy the whole environmental surroundings for years as a huge area will become radioactive, people and animals will suffer from the consequences for years. Therefore uranium is another highly dangerous element.

Evaluation

4 This article appeared in the British newspaper ...

Verweis auf *Useful phrases* zu *A letter to the editor* (S. 22/S. 48).

Lösungsvorschlag

Dear Mr Russel,
Your article about "carbon credit cards" attracted my interest at once. Pollution and the greenhouse effect have become dominating topics in worldwide politics. Therefore any suggestion to reduce the emissions of carbon should be taken seriously. Still the idea of your article seems to contain a lot of difficulties and might be hard to realise. It is true that individual carbon emission must be restricted. I doubt, however, that carbon as a new "currency" would be accepted by the majority of the population. Therefore I think we should begin to concentrate on the small measures that can be taken in the short term before we invent new ways of reducing carbon emissions. If more people knew about the easy ways of saving energy we would probably not need any "carbon credit cards" at all.
Sincerely yours,

Text production

5 Creative writing

Lösungsvorschlag

Everything started in the United States. Some years ago the United States was the only country not to sign the Kyoto declaration. Now everything has changed. As one of the first countries the United States accepted that pollution and climate change were too dangerous for mankind and its environment. Therefore the US government developed a new currency system. Everybody got a certain amount of carbon dioxide he or she could spend during one year. Everything could be paid in carbon dioxide credit points. For environmental crimes one had to pay penalty carbon points. Driving cars and flying airplanes became very expensive as the unnecessary emissions of carbon dioxide was supposed to be declining. Saving energy had become the most important goal of the American population and everybody joined in this campaign.

3
Saving the planet   Red alert! Climate change takes it toll on Scotland

Frank began to feel desperate. The month had just begun and he had already wasted all of his carbon credit points. He was basically not good enough at saving energy to survive with this new currency. Everything had become so expensive. Driving his car for example …

Newspaper article   **Red alert! Climate change takes it toll on Scotland**   pp. 26/27

HINTERGRUNDINFO

The article by **Ian Johnston** in "The Scotsman" started a debate on the Internet about environment protection and climate change in Scotland. On the one hand people believe that their mother country is too small to have an effect on climate change, on the other hand there are supporters who agree with Professor Colin Galbraith that everyone can do his/her bit to reduce or prevent the negative effects of climate change.

The Scottish Environment Protection Agency (SEPA) is Scotland's environmental regulator and adviser. It is responsible to the Scottish Parliament through ministers. The agency was established by the Environment Act in 1995 and works with many other organisations to help protect and improve the environment. It has about 1,200 employees working at different locations all over Scotland.
Its objectives are:

– to achieve of good water, air and land quality,
– to help with the minimisation and recovery of waste,
– to protect, inform and involve communities,
– to promote economic well-being.

Dr Campbell Gemmell was appointed chief executive of SEPA in 1994.

The Scottish Natural Heritage (SNH) is one of the biggest assets in Scotland and as a governmental body responsible to ministers of the Scottish government. It was established in 1992 and its major aim is to care for and protect the natural heritage through the provision of grants and licenses, research projects, advice and information, and publications. The SNH is a corporation and works nationally and locally in so-called "units", which have offices all over Scotland.

Lernwortschatz   red alert, to be responsible for sb/sth, level, sea level, to be up by X%, long-term, impact, to be under threat from sb/sth, urbanisation, to halt the loss of sth, the debate focuses on sth

Materialien   → Online-Link: 601002-0008

Research   **1 Collect information about the geography …**

Verweis auf *Fact file* zu *Scotland*. Die S präsentieren die gesammelten Informationen als PowerPoint-Präsentation oder in Form von Postern oder Plakaten. L: *Present your knowledge in an attractive (for your fellow students) form.*

Lösungsvorschlag   The climate in Scotland is temperate and very changeable, but not extreme. Scotland has a large coastline with a lot of islands, many rivers and small lakes called lochs. Many parts of Scotland are very mountainous. The highest point is Ben Nevis with 1344 metres. Other parts of Scotland are covered with big forests and a variety of wildlife. The economy is dominated by steel and shipping industries as well as coal mining. Sheep breeding is one of the main agricultural businesses.

Comprehension   **2 Make a list of all the areas of the environment …**

Die S fertigen die Listen in Einzelarbeit an und beziehen die Informationen der *Fact file* und das Foto auf S. 26 mit ein.

3 | Saving the planet — Red alert! Climate change takes it toll on Scotland

Lösungsvorschlag	Affected areas	Effects
	• endangered species • rising sea levels • biodiversity • rainfall pattern • rising levels of winter rain, heavier rainfall • storms, drier soils • temperature • wind and storm events • land-use changes, urbanisation	• decline challenging, loss of island nesting seabird populations • major floods • habitat loss, spread of non-native species • wetter • severe river flooding, affecting 77,000 homes and buildings • landslides • warmer, flowers three weeks earlier, rise in sea temperatures • coastal erosion • some species reduced, other extended

Analysis 3 Analyse the means that are used ...

Die S fertigen die Analyse schriftlich in Einzelarbeit als **Hausaufgabe** an. Die Aufgabenstellung eignet sich gut als Vorübung für eine vergleichbare Aufgabenstellung in einer Klausur.

Lösungsvorschlag
- Reliable sources (type of newspaper; environmental watchdog SEPA, ll. 3/4; State of Scotland's Environment 2006 report, l. 9; research, l. 29; Dr Campbell Gemmell, l. 40; Professor Colin Galbraith, director, ll. 45/46).
- Figures/concrete examples (rise of sea level off Aberdeen: 0.66 mm per year, ll. 13/14; rise of temperatures: one degree C/40 years, ll. 15/16; snowdrops, daffodils flowered three weeks earlier, l. 32; affecting 77,000 houses, l. 35; 99,000 species, l. 43).

Discussion 4 Discuss whether the results of SEPA could be true ...

Lösungsvorschlag
The results of the greenhouse effect are not only a Scottish phenomenon, but concern the environment worldwide. Therefore the results of SEPA could not only be true in Germany as well, but take place at any moment. As the variety of flora and fauna in Scotland might be higher than it is in Germany it is less alarming. There are, however, news of dying forests, lakes drying out and fewer animals every day. The report SEPA had published does not only concern the Scottish environment but is part of the alarming worldwide trend of global warming. Therefore it concerns every country and region in the same way.

Evaluation 5 Report

Die Aufgaben 4 und 5 können gemeinsam behandelt und als **Hausaufgabe** ausgearbeitet werden. In der Folgestunde erfolgt ein kurzer Vortrag (5–8 Minuten) unter Verwendung geeigneter Medien (Folie/PowerPoint-Präsentation/Grafik/Diagramm).

Lösungsvorschlag
Not only in other countries, but also in Germany the average temperature has risen during recent years. As a result of the rising sea level, parts of German islands have been flooded. People there have had to leave their houses and move further away from the coast. In connection with agriculture, bad harvests are the consequence of long periods of rain or long times without any rain. Thus corn becomes rare and leads to higher prices for important products like bread for example. Both, farmers who lose their income and people who buy the bread are affected in the same way.

Saving the planet Global warming profits 3

Discussion **6 The fact file on Scotland mentions the 3 R's for ecology …**

Lösungsvorschlag *Especially plastic waste can easily be recycled. Therefore a lot of households separate their waste. At my house for example we have four different bins in the kitchen. One is for biological products, the other one contains only paper. The third one is the above mentioned plastic bin. Everything that doesn't fit into any of the three goes into the fourth bin. This is how we recycle. A lot of things are, however, reused, like plastic bags for example. And we try to reduce the waste of energy by switching off every light when we leave rooms and use the car only when it is necessary. I reckon recycling is most important. A lot of things can neither be reduced nor be reused. By separating waste, however, we can take part in the recycling system which helps to reduce and reuse at the same time.*

Project work **7 [👥] Project "Adaptation" …**

Das Projekt kann in Zusammenarbeit mit dem Fach Biologie erfolgen. Informationen über ausgestorbene Tiere sind u.a. erhältlich auf der Website des Informationszentrums Chemie Biologie Pharmazie (Engelbert Zass): www.infochembio.ethz.ch/links/zool_prehistor.html sowie auf *The Extinction Website* (Peter Maas): http://extinctanimals.petermaas.nl/.

Lösungsvorschlag
- *Examples for species of plant or animal that have adapted well: cactus, carnivores (dt. Fleischfresser); penguin, chameleon.*
- *Examples for extinct plant or animal: Cooke's Kokia (Hawaiian Islands), Usambara Mountain Tree (extinct 1910, Tanzania), Eboracia (extinct in the Jurassic Era); mammoth (extinct approx. 11,000 years ago), elephant bird (dt.: Elefantenvogel, extinct approx. 1,000 years ago), Dire wolf (extinct approx. 16,000 years ago), Tasmanian tiger (dt. Beutelwolf, extinct 1936), Guam Flying Fox (dt. Guam Flughund, extinct 1968).*

Erweiterung Alternatives Projekt: *Collect information about other regions in the English-speaking world (e.g. California), depict their ecological situation and how it is dealt with.* Mögliche Themen:
- Geografie (*area: 424,002 km², population: 38 million, National Parks, etc.*),
- Ökonomie,
- Umwelt (u.a. www.ecorazzi.com),
- *Internet hype* (*Silicon Valley, talent density,* siehe Themenheft, S. 10/11),
- Geschichte,
- Hollywood (*3rd biggest employer*),
- *California songs*,
- Forschung (*university, solar power in Dagget, wind power on Montezuma Hills*),
- Auszüge aus T.C.Boyles "The Tortilla Curtain" über Buschbrände und Erdrutsche (*Part 3: Socoppo*),
- "The Green Giant" (*Newsweek*, 16/4/2007, *US-Edition* über Arnold Schwarzenegger als Umweltaktivist),
- Georgetown University Environmental Conference "Governor's Remarks" (Rede Schwarzeneggers zu *climate change* und Maßnahmen),
- Kalifornien. Das bessere Amerika, in: Stern Nr. 10, 28/2/08 (interessante Informationen).

Die ersten acht Punkte (Geografie bis Forschung) können als S-Vorträge aufbereitet werden. Als Ausgangspunkt für die Diskussion eignet sich das Zitat von Truman Capote: *"It's a scientific fact that if you stay in California you lose one point of your IQ every year."*

Newspaper article **Global warming profits** p. 28

HINTERGRUNDINFO

Al Gore (born 1948) started his career as a military reporter in the Vietnam War and as a journalist in Tennessee, which is also the state where he grew up. His political career includes member of the US House of Representatives and the US Senate. He was the candidate for the Democratic Party in the presidential elections in 2000. His loss against George W. Bush was followed by a

3 Saving the planet Global warming profits

controversy over the election results in Florida, which finally made the candidate of the Republicans president of the US. After his political career Al Gore is now popular and known all over the world as an environmental activist. The documentary "An Inconvenient Truth" (2005) by Davis Guggenheim introduces Al Gore, his personal objectives and achievements, and documents his campaign for environment protection. In 2007 Al Gore won the Nobel Peace Prize for his campaigns and his efforts regarding environment protection.

***Davis Guggenheim** (born 1964): American film director and producer, who won the Academy Award for best documentary feature in 2007 for his documentary "An Inconvenient Truth".*

***"An Inconvenient Truth"** (2006) is a documentary based on a show presented by Al Gore about global warming and was a worldwide success winning an Academy Award in 2007.*

Lernwortschatz *to give sb his/her due, single-handedly, pending, sustainability, environmentalist, to pay off for sb, fossil fuel, alternative energy*

Materialien → Online-Link: 601002-0009

Discussion Verweis auf die *VIP file* zu *Al Gore* (S. 29). L-Impuls: *Look at the photo and brainstorm on what you know about Al Gore. Then analyse the diagram and comment on its findings.*
Mögliche Lösung:
- *Two graphs showing the rise of temperatures worldwide.*
- *Temperatures are rising steadily.*
- *Natural development vs. man-made climate change.*

Alternative Die S schauen die Dokumentation als Einstieg und bearbeiten zuerst den deutschsprachigen Artikel auf S. 29. Danach folgt der Zeitungsartikel auf S. 28 zur Vertiefung.

Comprehension ## 1 Describe Al Gore and his activities

Erweiternde Fragestellung nach der Beschreibung: *What is your opinion about his activities?*

Lösungsvorschlag
- *Former US Vice-president.*
- *Author of "An Inconvenient Truth".*
- *Warns of effects of climate change.*
- *Initiated "Live Earth".*
- *Shrewd businessman.*
- *Co-founder of an investment fund.*

Analysis ## 2 Make a list of striking terms used in this text …

Verweis auf *Useful phrases* zu *Discussing the tone.*

Lösungsvorschlag
- *eco hero*
- *pocket-lining opportunist*
- *the Goracle*
- *pop music glitterati*
- *epic global alarmfest*
- *fat profits*

Influence on the tone of the article: The tone is very ironical, at times even sarcastic, see ll. 10/11: "… revered environmentalists as Madonna and The Red Hot Chili Peppers." (Students might refer to the environmental damage that the 2007 concerts caused.) The tone causes us to think whether Al Gore can be seen from a different, more critical point of view as well.

Saving the planet   Eine unbequeme Wahrheit   **3**

Evaluation **3 Comment on the question asked at the end …**

Die Aufgabe eignet sich als vorbereitende Übung auf eine spätere Klausur zu dem Themenkomplex. Sie sollte deshalb in Einzelarbeit als **Hausaufgabe** erledigt werden.

Lösungsvorschlag *Reflecting on environmental protection has much to do with financial topics. Either such as the idea of using carbon as a new currency or such as Al Gore earning money with his publicity for environmental protection. I am absolutely convinced that the growing fear of the greenhouse effect, global warming and the desire for alternative energy stocks will become a big market for investors and companies. It is striking how many new subjects concerning alternative energies are offered by universities. Engineers can specialise in environmental protection, for example in the car industry. Soon this market and these jobs will not be anything special but part of worldwide capitalism and the global markets.*

Erweiterung Weiterführende Aufgabenstellungen für Gruppenarbeitsphasen:
- *Do some research and write a fact file on environmental sustainability.* Ggf. Hinweis auf www.sustain.canterbury.ac.nz. Mögliche Lösung:
  Environmental sustainability is the ability to maintain the qualities that are valued in the physical environment. It means managing the use, development and protection of natural and physical resources in a way, or at a rate, which enables people and communities to provide for their social, economic and cultural well-being and for their health and safety.
- *Do some research on alternative or so-called green technology businesses and stocks. What kind of "clean" energy do they rely on? Are they profitable?* Ggf. Hinweis auf *WilderHill Clean Energy Index*, www.wildershares.com/. Mögliche Lösung (siehe auch S. 42, Antwort zu Themenheft, Seite 24, Aufgabe 1):
  Examples can be found in the following fields: fuel cell makers, solar/hydrogen power firms, wind/tidal power and biomass energy outfits, plug-in hybrid vehicles (still rather risky businesses but interest in these businesses is soaring).

Magazine article ### Eine unbequeme Wahrheit   p. 29

Lernwortschatz *elections, circumstance, vote, global warming, lecture, director, motive, vain self-display, unavoidable, achievement, entertaining, waste separation, to preach to the choir (AE)/to the converted (BE), reduction of greenhouse gases, progressive, awareness*

1 Mediation

Lösungsvorschlag *Recycling waste is part of the German daily routine. Driving our cars has become very expensive as a result of high petrol prices and nearly everyone tries to save energy in order to reduce carbon emissions. Therefore Al Gore's movie "An Inconvenient Truth" does not tell the main part of the German population anything new. It is, however, another way of reminding people how bad the effects of pollution have become. In Germany people wonder what Al Gore's real aim is. Does he really want to save our planet or is he keen on publicity concerning himself? Summing up, I think "A Inconvenient Truth" is a good film to remind people of their duty to save the planet, but it does not deliver revolutionary new ideas.*

Evaluation #### 2 Writing a film review

L: *Discuss Al Gore's findings and arguments and the impact they might have on our environmental conscience. Take notes while watching the documentary to write a review later.* Die schriftliche Ausarbeitung des *review* kann als **Hausaufgabe** erfolgen. L gibt dazu bei Bedarf noch einige Hinweise. L: *How to write a film review? Info about the film, intro (expectations, background), genre & theme, plot (don't reveal the end), characters, director, soundtrack, general review/recommendation, rating.*

49

3 | Saving the planet — Eine unbequeme Wahrheit

Lösungsvorschlag

"An Inconvenient Truth" is a documentary that tries to show possible consequences of global warming. Many of the topics Al Gore dealt with are not new for the main part of the Europeans. For Americans, who did not sign the Kyoto protocol, "An Inconvenient Truth" might offer completely new consequences of global warming. The movie is a mixture of proved facts and sarcasm. It shows a lot of passion for environmental protection. The message of the movie is obvious, it can be easily understood. So easily that you sometimes get the impression you are watching an advertisement.

Evaluation

3 Look at the cartoon ...

Der schriftliche *comment* bietet sich ebenfalls als **Hausaufgabe** an.

Lösungsvorschlag

The cartoon shows a man who claims that overpopulation and pollution are responsible for a development that will destroy civilisation. He is dressed according to this opinion and has long hair and a beard. His whole appearance shows how much he despises the general idea of civilisation. In my opinion we don't need people who only draw a pessimistic image of our future without offering ideas on how to improve the situation. All these people do is claim how much worse things have become and look for the reasons without thinking of solutions. What we need are people who point at the problems and know about the difficulties and effects of pollution and the misuse of energy resources but try to work against this development at the same time.

Erweiterung

Zur Bewusstmachung der Konnotationen werden die wichtigsten Termini an die Tafel geschrieben. Die S halten ihre Assoziationen schriftlich fest (Partner-/Gruppenarbeit). Mögliche Lösung:

The language of the environment fight

Terms used	Connotations, associations, comment
Global warming	Catastrophic. Puts the focus on worldwide average temperature. Only works for half the year. Leaves out regional dangers of storms, floods and drought. Is not a crisis.
Climate change	In the US, consistent with Republican practice, which calls for deemphasising the urgency of the situation. Sounds controllable, not emotional.
Greenhouse effect	Most common term in the early 1980s. Puts emphasis only the mechanism, namely the build-up of heat-trapping gases in the atmosphere – but not on the outcome.
Climate crisis	Favoured by Al Gore and sceptic Michael Crichton (the novelist). Immediate action is needed. Conveys the notion that this is hopeless.
Climate chaos	Favoured in Europe. Translates as "Klimakatastrophe".

Alternative terms: environmental heating, thermal catastrophe, worldwide calorification, atmospheric pyrogenesis, planetary emergency, meteorological calamity.

Weitere mögliche Aufgabenstellungen:
- *Discuss the associations and connotations of the terms used and point out your opinion. Which term do you prefer?*
- *Check some German newspapers and find out how often the above – conventional – terms are used, by whom and to what effect.*
- *Analyse the "alternative terms" and comment on their reasonability.*
- *Discuss whether they will ever be used by a broad public.*

Saving the planet — A friend of the earth   3

Alternative L: *Together with a partner give a short definition and a translation of the terms below. Study different German newspapers and add in which context and how frequently they are used. Complete the table.*

Term	Translation	Usage, associations, comment
Global warming		
Climate change		
Greenhouse effect		
Climate crisis		
Climate chaos		

Novel excerpt   **A friend of the earth**   pp. 30/31

HINTERGRUNDINFO

T.C. Boyle (Thomas Coraghessan Boyle), born in 1948, is an American novelist and short story writer. Since the late 1970s he has published many novels and more than 60 short stories and won several awards for his writing.

"A Friend of the Earth" (2000): Boyle's dystopian fiction tells the story of Tyrone Tierwater, who joined the environment protection movement in the 1990s and was convicted for eco-terrorism. In 2025 he meets his ex-wife Andrea again, whose friend wants to write a story about Ty's daughter Sierra who died a martyr fighting to save trees. Tierwater is confronted with his past and reflects about his behaviour as eco-activist. The novel questions whether environmental protection really makes sense or if the individual's actions are just meaningless. The novel received very good reviews. On T.C. Boyle's interactive website you can get in touch with the author on his message board.

Friends of the Earth International is the largest grassroots environmental network worldwide whose major aim is to create and maintain a safe and healthy environment. In order to achieve that, numerous campaigns on all continents are initiated considering the issues of global warming, transportation, energy, nutrition and many more. Friends of the Earth International has member organisations from 70 nations (including Germany's BUND) and more than 5,000 local activists groups worldwide.

Lernwortschatz *to rank in/among, precious little, for the record, to be dimly aware of sth, consciousness, to abuse, to get around to (doing) sth, packaging, to conserve, global warming, fuel, landfill, permanent, attic, trunk, neat, to assume, approximately, to see the light, to put sth in motion, glacier*

Discussion L-Impulse: *Look at the pictures on p. 31. Brainstorm on what you have heard about "tree people". What place do you think of when you look at the photo on the right?* L kann einen oder zwei S beauftragen, dem Kurs T.C. Boyle in Form einer Kurzpräsentation vorzustellen: *The life and works of T.C. Boyle.*

1 Mediation

Lösungsvorschlag *A friend of the earth* ist ein Roman, der im Jahr 1990 und 2025 spielt. Der Erzähler ist in dem Textauszug 75 Jahre alt und vom Leben sehr enttäuscht. Er ist zu einem Menschenfeind geworden. Es ist sein erklärtes Ziel, die bereits stark zerstörte Umwelt zu retten. In dem vorliegenden Textauszug erklärt er, wie er früher gelebt hat und wie sehr alles, was er früher getan hat, der Umwelt geschadet hat. Er hält sich und alle anderen Menschen für Verbrecher. Er hat daraufhin sein Leben radikal geändert und sich der Umweltschutzgruppe *Earth Forever* angeschlossen. Er sagt sich von sämtlichen Dingen los, die mit seinem früheren Leben zusammenhängen.

3 | Saving the planet A friend of the earth

Comprehension

2 Make a grid to compare Ty's and ...

Zusatzmaterial → Kopiervorlage 6 (Environmentally sinning)

Lösungsvorschlag a)

Ty's behaviour	My own and my family's behaviour
Wasted energy (oil heating).	Waste energy (heating, electricity, etc.).
	Or don't because house is insulated, save energy (reduce heating, switch off unneeded appliances, no standby).
Abused the resources of the earth.	Waste water (bath, shower, water the lawn, etc.).
Did not recycle (except twice a year).	Recycle all the time.
Drove fast, wasted fuel.	Reduce usage of car, go by bike, public transport instead.
Polluted the environment.	Occasionally throw away paper or packaging, other waste.

b) T.C. Boyle's accusation that I am a criminal can be seen from two different points of view. On the one hand I do not feel like a criminal at all. I don't think I've ever done anything criminal except small things like driving too fast for example. Therefore without reading the whole text and only reacting on his claim I would say that T.C. Boyle is wrong in calling his readers criminals. Reflecting on his statement in lines 43–45 one could begin to agree with his opinion. He is right if he says that every citizen of the Western World produces a great amount of environmental pollution. Concerning the effect of pollution it is therefore true to call me a criminal rather than any individual living in a Third World country. It is even truer if we consider that T.C. Boyle is mainly addressing American citizens. Not signing the contract of Kyoto, America is the biggest producer of carbon emissions and a lot of its citizens can be called criminals in connection with environmental protection.

Erweiterung Zum Abschluss dieses Abschnitts kann **Kopiervorlage 6** (Seite 98) eingesetzt werden. Das Arbeitsblatt bietet den S die Möglichkeit, anhand eines detaillierten Tagesplans herauszufinden, welche der alltäglichen persönlichen Umweltsünden vermeidbar sind.

Analysis

3 Discuss the tone of the text ...

Aufgabe a) wird im Plenum diskutiert, Aufgabe b) kann als schriftliche **Hausaufgabe** gestellt werden.

Lösungsvorschlag a) *Examples of sarcasm, simile and word choice:*
- Let's eat each other, … (l. 7)
- Ecology. What a joke. (l. 8)
- … three-thousand-square-foot house (l. 12)
- … oil burner the size of Texas (l. 13)
- … commune with the squirrels (l. 16)
- … like a permanent filling in a rotten tooth (l. 24)
- … like filings to a magnet (l. 25)
- … like a napkin dispenser in a restaurant (l. 35)
- … tattered, bleeding planet (l. 46)
- … may he rot in hell … (l. 49)

Influence on the tone: The exaggerations make you smile at first, but when you start to think about the deeper sense of the statements you are impressed.

b) *My daily part of destroying nature*
This morning when I woke up I realised that I had forgotten to switch off the TV last night. But I didn't really care because it is switched on the whole day anyway. After a short breakfast I went upstairs to take a shower. At least twenty minutes every morning. I couldn't start a working day without having a long hot shower in the morning. Although it would be cheaper to go by bus to work I took my car. It is true that the car causes environmental pollution but it's easier and more relaxing. I am definitely one of those people who don't care much about the environment. I am

Saving the planet **A friend of the earth** **3**

just not interested in this topic. Sometimes I feel a bit guilty about that, but normally it doesn't last long. It is too exhausting to think about it. I'd rather be an environmental criminal than use my bike, do without my showers or remember to switch off my TV.

Evaluation

4 *Comment on the last sentence (lines 60–61).*

Lösungsvorschlag

Boyle's way of presenting humans is very pessimistic. The last sentence shows how much T.C. Boyle's first person narrator despises mankind for its way of treating the earth and the environment. According to his opinion humans will destroy the earth without having the chance of protecting it. I think this statement is too absolute and too pessimistic. It is true that humans are the biggest threat to the environment. But we all have to come to terms with our duty to protect the earth as well. We cannot ignore it. If we were an enemy of the people, we would have to be an enemy of ourselves. In my opinion we have to try to be both, a friend of the earth but also a friend of the people. I think this is possible and we can manage it.

Text production

5 *Read reviews of the book ...*

Lösungsvorschlag

"A friend of the Earth" is an interesting novel about environmental problems. I doubt, however, that you would like this novel. The whole atmosphere is hopeless and depressive. According to T.C. Boyle and his first person narrator we don't have a chance to change this development. Furthermore, the two narrative perspectives and two plots with a gap of 35 years in between make it difficult to read. Moreover, you really have to like science fiction novels and you have to be interested in environmental problems as well. I wonder whether you might like these two aspects of "A friend of the Earth". If you still decide to read it, you'll have to be prepared that it is not a novel you can easily read and then forget about. It will make you think about this topic and probably even depress you as well.

Research

6 [💻] *Consult the Internet to find out ...*

Verweis auf *Useful phrases* zu *Talking about short films.* Die Vorbereitung erfolgt in Einzelarbeit zu Hause. In der nächsten Stunde werden einige Arbeitsergebnisse im Plenum präsentiert.

Lösungsvorschlag

There are some short movies by "Friends of the Earth" that can be found on the Internet. One of them seems to cover most of the organisation's ideas. This movie is a mixture of a cartoon and a documentary and is very informative. A narrator explains the ideas of the organisation while many pictures referring to the topic try to attract the reader's attention. The movie is not funny or impressive but can be used as a good advertisement for "Friends of the Earth" to explain the organisation's aims.

Research

7 [👥] *There are a lot of movements to do something ...*

Verweis auf *Useful phrases*, Seite 55/56.

Lösungsvorschlag

Movements for the protection of the environment:
Worldwide Fund for Nature (WWF), Greenpeace, Bund für Umwelt und Naturschutz Deutschland (BUND), Naturschutzbund Deutschland (NABU), *etc.*

I reckon all of them worthy of my support. If I had to decide which of them I'd rather support I think WWF and Greenpeace are really interesting. They are active worldwide and especially Greenpeace often openly does battle against environmental crimes. They fight against big companies and always have great ideas to protect the environment. WWF is more peaceful than Greenpeace but as one of the biggest international environmental organisations it is definitely worth supporting. So are the German organisations but because of their special interest in Germany's environment I'd rather support the organisations acting worldwide.

53

3 | Saving the planet Severn Suzuki speaks in Rio

Video clip | **[5◉] Severn Suzuki speaks in Rio** | p. 32

HINTERGRUNDINFO

*One year after her success in Rio **Severn Cullis-Suzuki**'s book "Tell the World" was published in which she gives advice to families on how to live an environmentally friendly life. She received a degree in ecology and evolutionary biology from Yale and became a member of Kofi Annan's special Advisory Panel. In 2000 the Internet-based think tank "Skyfish Project" was launched, which has since then been successful in initialising new projects. In 2002 Suzuki went to the UN World Summit on Sustainable Development in Johannesburg presenting a document called the "Recognition of Responsibility".*

Lernwortschatz — *to change one's way, hidden agenda, on behalf of sb, to go unheard, cancer, to go extinct, to vanish, species, privileged, greedy, tremendous, victim of war, list of priorities, to challenge sb*

Materialien — → CD, Track 5

Comprehension | ### 1 Listen to the speech and write down …

[5◉] | Bevor Aufgabe 1 bearbeitet wird, spielt L **Track 5** zweimal von der CD-ROM vor.

Lösungsvorschlag | **a)** *I was deeply impressed about the way a twelve-year-old girl expressed herself. It is not the naïve speech of a child, every word is wisely chosen and fits perfectly into the context. The most impressive thing is, however, the way Severn Suzuki speaks: The audience understands that she really means what she says and that she is trying to convince her audience especially with her enormous background knowledge of this topic.*
b) *Severn Suzuki is right when she claims that nobody knows how to repair nature once it has been destroyed. She tells her audience that nobody can fix the ozone layer, nor can anyone bring back vanished animals or whole forests. This is the most convincing argument: as soon as nature is destroyed it cannot be rebuilt.*

Analysis | ### 2 Make a list of all the rhetorical devices …

Lösungsvorschlag

Parallelism	*"I am here to speak …"*
	"I am afraid to go out/to breathe …"
	"We are afraid to share/let go …"
Rhetorical question	*"Did you have to worry of these little things when you were my age?"*
	"Then why do you go out and do the things you tell us not to do?"
	"Are we even on your list of priorities?"
	"Why are we … so greedy?"
Direct address	*"… but I want you to realise, neither do you!"*
	"… you teach us how to behave in the world."
	"You grown-ups say you love us …"
Enumeration	*"We have watches, bicycles, computers and television sets."*
Climax	*"And you can't bring back the forests that once grew …"*
	"… you are someone's child."
Repetition	*"I'm only a child…"*
	"We buy and throw away …"
Quotation	*"I wish I was rich …"*
	"You are what you do …"

Effectiveness: *The rhetorical devices Suzuki uses in her speech make the audience listen to her arguments carefully. She is very convincing through her vividness, strong appeal and authenticity.*

Saving the planet   Let's not worry about climate change!   3

Text production

3 Write a letter to Suzuki telling her ...

Lösungsvorschlag *Dear Severn Suzuki,*

When I heard a child was going to speak at the Rio Earth Summit I wondered whether any adult would take a child's sorrows seriously and how the reactions to your speech would be. Furthermore, I wondered whether a twelve-year-old girl had the strength to speak at a conference like the Rio Earth Summit. I was, however, deeply impressed when I listened to your speech. It was amazing how clearly you pronounced every word without any fear of all the people in front of you. It was even more amazing how convincingly you put across your message to the audience. With your speech you touched every single man and woman at the Rio Earth Summit. So did you touch me and I agreed with every word you said to the audience. It is true we can't heal the world once it has been destroyed. It is true we are responsible for dying animals and rainforests. And it is furthermore true we all want our children to see how beautiful nature can be.

Best wishes,

Evaluation

4 [👥] Role play

Lösungsvorschlag

Reporter:	*Do you think the Rio Earth Summit is the right place for a twelve-year-old girl to give a speech about environmental pollution?*
Conference participant:	*To be honest I was a bit sceptically at first but the more I listened to this amazing girl the more I realised how important it is to listen to the children's arguments.*
Reporter:	*But don't you think a specialist's arguments would have been more convincing to the audience than the speech of a child?*
Conference participant:	*Not at all. I think everybody was impressed and deeply touched by the girl's speech. We all understood that she really meant what she said. Look around, she got a standing ovation.*
Reporter:	*Do you think we will remember this speech one day?*
Conference participant:	*We definitely will. Hopefully it opened people's minds and we can soon start to reduce the worldwide waste of energy and start a new age of environmental protection. This girl might be the symbol for this new movement.*

Research

5 Find out about other summit meetings and report on one in class.

Lösungsvorschlag *In 2002 there was another Earth Summit in Johannesburg, South Africa. It resulted in the Johannesburg declaration that included decisions and explanations on how to fight hunger, HIV, organised crime and natural disasters for example. The US as one of the most important countries, however, was not present at all.*

Advertisement

Let's not worry about climate change!   p. 33

HINTERGRUNDINFO

The Observer: *Serious broadsheet Sunday paper of the Guardian Group, left-wing to middle-of-the-road.*

Sir Montgomery Cecil, *name of a made-up industrialist, aviator and President of SPURT, is convinced that air traffic does not harm the environment and attacks environmentalists for their campaigning to stop climate change by reducing travelling by plane. He calls for a political leader who is indifferent to environmental issues and climate change and believes Gordon Brown to be perfect in*

that role (cf. plans of government to expand British airports). This is why Cecil, using the slogan "Why go green, when you have Brown?", started a campaign to support the prime minister and strengthen the air industry.

Terminal 5 (T5) *of Heathrow Airport was opened by Queen Elizabeth on 14 March 2008, owned by BAA (British Airports Authority) and exclusively used by British Airways (BA).*

3 | Saving the planet Let's not worry about climate change!

Lernwortschatz *climate change, aviation, environmentalist, to be cowed, green tax, in sb's back yard*

Comprehension ## 1 Make sure you understand these words and phrases ...

Diese Aufgabe kann auch in Partnerarbeit erfolgen.

Lösungsvorschlag *stuff* – vergiss es
spurt – Spurt, Sprint
lentil mob – Körnerfresser
can – halblang machen
be cowed – eingeschüchtert, in die Enge getrieben
reject out of hand – abwinken
whinger – Weichei, Jammerlappen
NIMBY – nicht mit mir
sod them – scheiß drauf

Tone and register: *Informal and vulgar in parts, very low register.*

Discussion ## 2 Describe and comment on the SPURT logo.

Verweis auf *Useful phrases* zu *Describing graphic elements*. Die S beschreiben die grafischen Komponenten der Anzeige unter Einbezug des Bildes und kommentieren sie. Die Anzeige wurde von Gegnern des Flughafenausbaus als Satire gestaltet und vollständig überzeichnet.

Lösungsvorschlag *Upwards movement of the elements implies the direction of the development. Underlines the clear, straight-forward text message.*

The SPURT logo shows two stripes that lead to an airplane and a text above that tries to convince people to forget about pollution and keep on travelling by airplane. The logo describes quite well what SPURT is trying to focus on. They ignore the environmental risks and motivate people to fly. Whether one agrees with the ideas of SPURT or not is another question, the logo itself definitely represents the organisation very well. At the same time, opponents of the aviation industry might point out that the vapour trail left by the airplane in the logo points to the pollution produced by airplanes.

Analysis ## 3 How would you describe the tone of this advertisement?

Die S befassen sich in einem Kursgespräch mit dem Text der Anzeige und bestimmen *tone* und *register* der Sprache. Anschließend Diskussion auf dem Hintergrund des Erscheinens im *Observer*.

Lösungsvorschlag *The tone of the advertisement is overbearing, aggressive, disdainful and, in parts, vulgar. With this aggressive stance, it is trying to appeal to concerned citizens in two ways. By pretending to want to attract the eye of the bosses of the aviation industry (as it is supposedly speaking about the environment as they do), it hopes to anger the thinking public. At the same time, its exaggerated stance toward both the environment and the aviation industry aim to provoke even the less thoughtful readers to pay attention to some of the facts they have written into the ad. The "Observer" may have both types of readers, so the ad will appeal to a wide group of people. It will also definitely get the casual reader's attention with its language, which would be unexpectedly vulgar for such a high-brow newspaper.*

Research ## 4 [👥] In groups, do some research on the plans ...

Die Arbeitsgruppen präsentieren ihre Ergebnisse in Form einer PowerPoint-Präsentation.

Saving the planet **Let's not worry about climate change!** **3**

Lösungsvorschlag *The British government has decided that it will be necessary to build more runways at London's airports. Around the year 2011 London-Stansted should get a second runway, shortly followed by a short new runway at London-Heathrow and a second runway at London-Gatwick. Therefore the SPURT's advertisement does not present wrong ideas but offers the right facts about the UK's plans for aviation.*

Discussion **5 [💻] *Go to the SPURT website and watch the video ...***

Die S diskutieren über Inhalt, Botschaft und die verwendeten Mittel in dem Videoclip.

Lösungsvorschlag *Message of the campaign:*
Fight the expansion of aviation in general and of the airports, gross way of protesting.
Means used in the campaign:
Saying/showing the exact opposite of what is aimed at, extremely exaggerated, shocking, laughter stuck in the throat, macabre.

Zusatzmaterial → **Klausurvorschlag 3 • Revision file 3**

Erweiterung • L kann als Vorbereitung auf Klausurvorschlag 3 den Auftrag erteilen: *Inform yourselves about Richard Branson's efforts to use bio fuels for flying.*
• Zum Abschluss des *Topics* füllen die S den zweiten Teil von *Revision file* 3 (Themenheft, Seite 61) aus. Ein Lösungsvorschlag befindet sich hier im Lehrerbuch (Seite 119).

4 | International peacekeeping Didaktisches Inhaltsverzeichnis

Topic 4: International peacekeeping

pp. 34–49

Didaktisches Inhaltsverzeichnis

Bearbeitungszeitraum: 19–22 Unterrichtsstunden

Textsorte/Thema	Unterrichts-methoden	Input boxes	Kompetenzen	Textproduktion
International peacekeaping			SB, Seite 34/35; LB, Seite 60–62	
Combination of visuals/The United Nations, global conflicts and strategies of peacekeeping	Kursgespräch Gruppenarbeit *Hot seat* Online-Link 14 Zusatzmaterial: Kopiervorlage 7	*Fact file: The United Nations* *Word bank: Talking about conflicts*	Orientierungswissen Recherchieren Gespräche führen Bildbeschreibung/-analyse	*Describing and assessing pictures*
[6⊚] Address at the Royal Institute of Int. Affairs, 2007 (700 words)			SB, Seite 36/37; LB, Seite 63–65	
Political speech/ The future of the UN	Kursgespräch Online-Link 15	*VIP file: Ban Ki-moon* *Tip: Examples of rhetorical devices* *Useful phrases: Talking about images* *Talking like a diplomat or politician*	Leseverstehen Hörverstehen	*Writing and giving a statement/speech*
[3🎞] An NGO at work, 2004 (65 words)			SB, Seite 38; LB, Seite 65–67	
Website/Non-governmental organisations	*Video transcript* (CD-ROM) Gruppenarbeit Online-Link 16	*Useful phrases: Talking about parts of a whole* *Fact file: A non-governmental organisation (NGO)*	Recherchieren Leseverstehen Hörverstehen Sehverstehen Gespräche führen Argumentieren	*Writing and giving a statement/speech* *Writing a newspaper article*
The world today – spotlight on Africa			SB, Seite 39; LB, Seite 67–70	
Political cartoon/ Africa: problems, conflicts, attractions	Gruppenarbeit Online-Link 17 Zusatzmaterial: Kopiervorlage 8/8a	*Fact file: African Union (AU)* *Useful phrases: Talking about negative feelings*	Sehverstehen Gespräche führen Argumentieren Recherchieren	*Giving a report Talking about a cartoon Describing and assessing a picture*
The USA – a global superpower (787 words)			SB, Seite 40; LB, Seite 70–73	
Combination of visuals (photos/ poster/cartoon)/ Global superpower USA, 9/11 and terrorism	*Video transcript* (CD-ROM) Kursgespräch Online-Link 18	*Useful phrases: Global roles*	Orientierungswissen Recherchieren Hörverstehen Sehverstehen Bildanalyse	*Describing and assessing a picture Viewing a docu-clip on the Internet*
[7⊚] Courtesy of the red, white and blue, 2002 (240 words)			SB, Seite 41; LB, Seite 73–76	
American song/ Mood and self-image of the US in 2002	Kursgespräch Online-Link 19	*Useful phrases: Talking about songs*	Hörverstehen Sehverstehen Leseverstehen Gespräche führen	*Talking about songs*

International peacekeeping   Didaktisches Inhaltsverzeichnis   **4**

Textsorte/Thema	Unterrichts-methoden	*Input boxes*	Kompetenzen	Textproduktion
America's role in the world: four options (327 words)			SB, Seite 42; LB, Seite 76–78	
Education programme/ America's global policy options	Gruppenarbeit Online-Link 20		Recherchieren Gespräche führen Argumentieren	*Describing a picture Giving a speech Conducting a panel discussion Making an interview*
Spot on facts, 2008 (520 words)			SB, Seite 43; LB, Seite 78–80	
American history: the US and the world		*Fact file on USA*	Orientierungswissen Leseverstehen	*Writing and giving a speech Writing a formal letter*
The opinion of the USA abroad, 2007			SB, Seite 44; LB, Seite 80/81	
Statistics/The global image of the US	Online-Link 21	*Useful phrases Useful phrases: Talking about image change*	Statistiken analysieren Recherchieren Gespräche führen Argumentieren	*Working with diagrams*
Germany's army, 2006 (326 words)			SB, Seite 45; LB, Seite 81–84	
Editorial/ Germany's global role	Kursgespräch	*Tip: Editorial (AE)/ leading article/leader (BE)*	Leseverstehen	*Writing and giving a speech Writing and giving a news item*
The European Union then and now, 2006 (281 words)			SB, Seite 46/47; LB, Seite 84–86	
Cartoons, map/The European Union: history, mission, global role	Kursgespräch Online-Link 22	*Useful phrases: Talking about problems Useful phrases: Talking about attitudes*	Orientierungswissen Recherchieren Leseverstehen Sehverstehen	*Talking about a cartoon Writing a dialogue Giving a speech*
[8/9 ◉] Two ambassadors' letters, 2007 (363 words)			SB, Seite 48; LB, Seite 87/88	
Letters to the editor/US–UK relationship, The UK and Europe		*Fact file: The UK and Europe Useful phrases: Writing a lettr to the editor*	Hörverstehen Leseverstehen Argumentieren	*Collecting arguments Writing a formal letter*
[10/11 ◉] The world in 2031, 2006 (308 words)			SB, Seite 49; LB, Seite 88–90	
Newspaper article/ Predictions for the world	*Tapescript (1060 words,* CD-ROM) Gruppenarbeit Zusatzmaterial: Klausurvor-schlag 4		Hörverstehen Leseverstehen	*Making a news programme*

4 | International peacekeeping Lead-in: International peacekeeping

Unterrichtsverlauf

Photos | **Lead-in: International peacekeeping** | pp. 34/35

HINTERGRUNDINFO

The United Nations *(in English abbreviated as "UN" and not "UNO") came into existence in 1945 when the five permanent members of the UN Security Council (China, France, Russian Federation, United Kingdom, and USA) agreed on the United Nations charter, the constituting instrument of the UN. It is the organisation's aim to work for peace and security in the world and to provide a foundation for a fruitful and respectful cooperation between all nations regarding international economic, social, cultural and humanitarian problems.*

The Security Council *with its five permanent and ten rotating members is the only organ of the UN which can make binding decisions (formulated as resolutions) that member governments have to carry out. The five permanent members have veto power, i.e. each of them can block the adoption of a resolution they find unacceptable. The ten additional seats are distributed on a regionally fair basis and rotate between the other member states every two years. The Security Council has been criticized for being unable to act effectively and quickly when confronted with a crisis, e.g. an act of aggression, genocide or human rights violations. The veto power of the five permanent member states, which often have opposing interests and aims, is often seen as the main cause of this problem. In addition, responsibility for the enforcement of its resolutions lies primarily with the Council members themselves, and there are often no consequences for violating a Security Council resolution. Some countries accuse the Security Council of partiality, e.g. of a pro-Arab bias in the Arab-Israeli conflict. The makeup of the Security Council dates back to the end of World War II, and this division of powers is often said to no longer represent the current realities of power in the world. Countries like Brazil, Germany, Japan and India are the first candidates for an extension of the number of permanent members.*

The Arab-Israeli conflict *originates in the Second World War when Jews were persecuted, sent to concentration camps, and killed all over Europe. After the war there was a general agreement by the United Nations to protect the Jewish people and make sure that the holocaust never happens again. As a compensation for the treatment of the Jews, it*

was the United Nations' aim to provide them with land where they could live in peace. Since the Jewish religion refers to Israel as the "holy land", the decision was made to give this land, which is surrounded by Muslim countries, to the Jews. However, at that time that region was inhabited by Palestinian Muslims who lived there since many of their holy places were also located in certain areas of that land, especially East Jerusalem. After fighting the Muslims in a war, Israel finally founded their own state in 1948. As a consequence, the Palestinian people consider the foundation of the state of Israel as an occupation of their land and regard the Israelis as invaders who have placed them under military rule. In order to defend themselves against the occupying forces, Palestinians built a terrorist network that continues to attack Israelis. The Israelis respond to the Palestinian terror with military force.

The Palestinians *feel restricted in their everyday lives due to the establishment of checkpoints by the Israelis between cities that Muslims have to pass through daily in order to go to work, visit their families or go shopping. Thus, the Palestinians experience the Israelis' control over their lives as an annoying hindrance to being a free people. The supply of water is also controlled by Israel, and Palestinians often do not have adequate access to water. Consequently, Palestinians feel abused and humiliated by the Israeli people. The building of Jewish settlements in Palestinian territory is another issue causing anger among the Palestinians.*

Israel *regards the Palestinian militants as terrorists who are a great danger to the Israelis. Its leaders do not trust Palestinian leaders and, therefore, a compromise is not seen as a plausible solution. Israel believes that it is necessary to continue its control over the Palestinian territories in order to protect itself. Since the beginning of the conflict there have been numerous suicide attacks in Israel killing many people and spreading fear and hatred towards the Palestinian peoples. Especially the towns that are close to the border suffer from Palestinian attacks and have to live with the threat of Muslim terrorism every day.*

| | International peacekeeping   Lead-in: International peacekeeping | **4** |

Lernwortschatz *the United Nations (UN), to convey, starting point, referee, historical, symbol, to found, victorious, world power, to aim to do sth, to promote, security, justice, economic, peacekeeping, humanitarian, member, veto power*

Materialien → Online-Link: 601002-0014

Discussion Einstieg in das Thema über globale Konfliktherde und die Rolle der UNO unter Verwendung von *various visuals (cartoon, poster, logo, photos).*

Visualising **1 *Use the visual elements above as a starting point ...***

Lösungsvorschlag Siehe **Hintergrundinfo** zu *United Nations,* S. 60.

Comprehension **2 *Read the fact file about the UN***

Lösungsvorschlag Individuelle S-Antworten.

Discussion **3 *Explain the symbolism of the flag of the UN ...***

Lösungsvorschlag a) ***Flag of the UN:*** *Introduced on 20 October 1947 – it shows the official emblem/logo of the United Nations in white, centred on a light blue ground and taking up half of the space – the emblem/logo consists of a projected map of the world as seen from above the North Pole with the continents in white and the water areas in light blue – it is surrounded by a wreath of olive branches.*
Symbolism: *The olive branches symbolise peace. The world map indicates the UN's aim of establishing peace and security worldwide.*

b) ***Historical context of the poster:*** *Towards the end of World War II the nations of the world united to fight Nazi Germany and its allies. The flags include those of the United States, Britain, Russia and France. The battle ships at the bottom signal that these nations are prepared to fight for freedom (and foreshadow the invasion of occupied Europe from the west). The poster anticipates the foundation of the United Nations in 1945 as an initiative of the victorious powers of World War II.*
Historical context of the cartoon: *In 2007, wars were fought in Afghanistan and Iraq. Neighbouring Iran under its leader Ahmadinejad supported Iraqi militias, made very critical remarks on the West, insisted on its right to use nuclear energy and even threatened to use nuclear weapons on Israel. The UN proved to be unable to control Iran's destabilising role in the Middle East.*

Alternative Die Aufgaben 1–3 können auch als vorbereitende **Hausaufgabe** gestellt und als Einstieg in das Thema im Plenum besprochen werden

Research **4 [👥👥] *Look at the world map ...***

Aufgabe **a)** wird im Plenum bearbeitet, die Aufgaben **b)** und **c)** erfolgen in arbeitsteiliger Gruppenarbeit zu vier Konflikten. Ergebnissicherung z.B. mit *one-page fact files* als *Handout/* Folie oder als Gruppenpräsentationen in Form eines Posters oder mediengestützt als PowerPoint-Präsentation.

Lösungsvorschlag a)/b) *e.g. China – Tibet, Afghanistan, Darfur, Serbia – Kosovo, Iran – UN*

c) *The Arab-Israeli conflict* (siehe **Hintergrundinfo**, S. 60)
Keywords: declaration of the state of Israel in 1947 – Palestinian refugees – controversial territories: the Gaza Strip, the Golan Heights, the West Bank, Jerusalem – Palestinians demand an independent state and refuse to accept a Jewish state – the division of Jerusalem with its holy places is the main obstacle to a peace settlement – broad international consensus that an

61

4 | International peacekeeping — Lead-in: International peacekeeping

independent Palestinian Arab state should be established within the areas occupied in 1967 – majorities among Israelis and Palestinians accept a two state solution, but Palestinians almost unanimously maintain the right of return of the refugees to Israel, and most Israelis oppose a Palestinian capital in East Jerusalem

Further current crises *(as of 2008) without short-term solutions:*

- *The war on terrorism in Iraq/Afghanistan: military presence vs. withdrawal of international troops/ethnic rivalry and anti-Western feelings/regional warlords/widespread infrastructure damage/terrorist activities and civil war/lack of democratic institutions/hope of national unity and peace/…*
- *The Kosovo conflict: political and territorial dispute up to 2007 a state under UN administration/declared independence in 2008/now a sovereign state (but legally still part of Serbia)/ongoing dispute over political status, autonomy and self-government.*
- *Turkey's policy of national unity vs. the Kurds' demand for an independent state: evacuation of villages/displacement/the Turkish military vs. the PKK/oppression and discrimination vs. revolts, terrorism and negotiations.*

Lernwortschatz *hot spot, conflict, conflicting, chance, diplomacy, preventive, intervention, mediation, confidence (in), negotiation, sanction, cease-fire, reconciliation, troops*

Evaluation
5 *Match the type of strategy with the examples.*

Anwendung von Handlungsoptionen auf aktuelle Konflikte. Aufgabe **a)** kann auch in Partnerarbeit erfolgen, Aufgabe **b)** wird im Kursgespräch behandelt.

Lösungsvorschlag   **a)** *1. – b): preventive diplomacy – early warnings, mediation, confidence building*
2. – e): military intervention – sending in troops, attacking another country
3. – c): negotiations, sanctions, cease-fire agreements
4. – a): placing peacekeeping forces between enemies
5. – d): peace-building – placing peacekeeping troo ps between enemies

b) *e.g. strategies/options for solving the Arab-Israeli conflict: sending in UN peacekeepers, cease-fire agreements, EU-led negotiations, etc.*

Discussion
6 [👥👥👥] *Hot seat*

Zusatzmaterial   → Kopiervorlage 7 (War and peace – words in context)

Mögliche Abfolge für eine argumentgestützte Diskussion zur Erarbeitung kontroverser Perspektiven:
1. Bildung von 3er-Gruppen,
2. Rollenzuweisung: *moderator/questioner – two representatives,*
3. Erstellen eines Ablaufplans mit Einstieg, Fragesequenz, Resümee,
4. Proben mit Reflektion (*parallel rehearsals*),
5. Zwei Präsentationen (evtl. auch mit Zuschauerfragen) und kriterienorientierter Vergleich/ Auswertung.

Lösungsvorschlag   *The Arab-Israeli conflict – opposing perspectives of the two conflicting parties:*
- *The Israelis see around them mostly undemocratic Arab states with underdeveloped economies, backward social standards and an aggressive religion, etc.*
- *The Arabs consider the Israelis colonial invaders and conquerors, who are aiming to control the entire Middle East, view Israel as a bridgehead for Western interference in the Middle East and feel general resentment concerning Israeli success and Arab failure, etc.*

Erweiterung   An dieser Stelle kann **Kopiervorlage 7** (Seite 99) zur Festigung der Lexik eingesetzt werden.

62

International peacekeeping · Address at the Royal Institute of International Affairs · **4**

Political Speech [6 ◎] **Address at the Royal Institute of International Affairs** p. 36

HINTERGRUNDINFO

Ban Ki-moon: At the time of his election as Secretary-General of the UN (1/1/2007), Ban Ki-moon was South Korea's Minister of Foreign Affairs and Trade. His long tenure with the Ministry included postings in New Delhi, Washington D.C. and Vienna, and responsibility for a variety of portfolios, including Foreign Policy Adviser to the President, Chief National Security Adviser to the President, Deputy Minister for Policy Planning and Director-General of American Affairs. Throughout this service, his guiding vision was that of a peaceful Korean peninsula, playing an expanding role for peace and prosperity in the region and the wider world.
Ban Ki-moon started his career after receiving a bachelor's degree in international relations from the Seoul National University in 1970. In the same year he entered the diplomatic service of his country, the Republic of South Korea. In 1985 he received his master's degree in public administration from Harvard. Since the beginning of his career as a diplomat, he has received numerous national and international prizes, medals and honours. His priorities as Secretary-General of the UN are peace and security, non-proliferation and disarmament, development, climate change, human rights and UN reform.

The Secretary-General represents the UN's ideals and functions as a spokesman of the people of the world, especially the poor and vulnerable. He is the "Chief administration officer" of the organisation, taking care of the member states' concerns. Therefore, he needs to keep in contact with the nations' leaders and representatives. It is the Secretary-General's task to try to prevent arguments arising and escalating between nations and react to misunderstandings or communication problems in his role as mediator between countries.

The Security Council proposes the Secretary-General, who is then elected by the General Assembly for a five-year term. It is possible to elect the same person again after this period as there is no restriction to the number of five-year terms.

The Royal Institute of International Affairs has been based at Chatham House for over 80 years. A prominent source of independent analysis and informed debate, its ideas on how to build a prosperous and secure world for everyone have a great influence in world politics.

Lernwortschatz *perception, to resolve, to outline, pressing, agenda, to step up, ongoing, to delay, cycle of violence, impact (on), to lack, joint, unprecedented, effort, core, concern, reconciliation, transition, refugee, disarmament, concerted, to pose, stalemate, to adopt, visionary*

Materialien → CD, Track 6 • Online-Link: 601002-0015

Comprehension **1** *Before you read: Scan the text ...*

Die Aufgabe kann (ggf. zusammen mit Aufgabe 2) als **Hausaufgabe** zu der Stunde gestellt werden. Möglicher Zwischenschritt als Hinführung zu Aufgabe 2: *Divide the speech into sections and give headings to each section. Note keywords to each section.*

Lösungsvorschlag *The world's most pressing global challenges in 2007:*
1. *the tragedy of Darfur (Sudan): cycle of violence (ll. 13–25),*
2. *the Middle East: the Arab-Israeli conflict, Iraq (ll. 26–37),*
3. *North Korea and Iran: political stalemate (ll. 38–44),*
4. *global terrorism (ll. 45–50).*

[6 ◎] Wird die Rede von der CD präsentiert, stellt L Aufgabe 1 zur Überprüfung des Globalverstehens nach dem ersten Vorspielen (Lösungsvorschlag siehe oben). Nach dem zweiten Hören von **Track 6** wird das Detailverstehen bei der Bearbeitung der weiteren Aufgaben überprüft.

Visualising **2** *Imagine Ban was using a projector to give listeners ...*

Die S präsentieren ihre Lösungsvorschläge auf Folie. Ein S hält die Rede foliengestützt in gekürzter Form frei.

63

4 | International peacekeeping   Address at the Royal Institute of International Affairs

Lösungsvorschlag

The UN and the world: challenges – perceptions – roles
The UN agenda in peace and security
Darfur: security and stability,
Middle East: progress in the question of Palestine,
Iraq: national reconciliation, reconstruction, development,
Iran: disarmament and non-proliferation,
Terrorism: counter-strategies.
The UN as a forum for a global agenda
Visionary and pro-active, dialogue and patience, resources and reform, peacekeeping and development, humanitarian work and human rights.

Analysis

3 Point out some rhetorical devices that Ban uses …

Verweis auf Tipp zu *Examples of rhetorical devices*. Hinführung zur Reaktivierung von Vorwissen: *How can a speaker rhetorically emphasise/illustrate his ideas and establish contact with his audience?* Die S finden und benennen die Beispiele im Text in Einzelarbeit, die Ergebnissicherung erfolgt im Kursgespräch.

Lösungsvorschlag

Rhetorical devices	Function/Effect
repetition of the keyword "challenge" (ll. 2, 5, 7)	emphasis/reinforcement
enumeration (l. 8)	emphasis on the future tasks
personal pronouns "we"/"I"	the UN as a whole vs. the personal responsibility of its leader
direct address/appeal (l. 5, 12, 41)	contact with listeners
colour imagery	diverse, controversial image of the UN
metaphor: cycle of violence (l. 15)	continuous, never-ending
rhetorical question (l. 46 ff.)	anticipates the listeners' question
anaphora (ll. 51–54)	emphasis on the future roles of the UN
double combination of two contradictory words (l. 59: double oxymoron in reversed order)	expresses the need for both support and (constructive) criticism
structuring	introduction (ll. 1–11) – main part (ll. 12–49) – conclusion (ll. 50–59)

One-minute statement

4 How does the UN work for peace in the world?

Hinführung erfolgt über die Besprechung des Vokabel-Inputs auf S. 37 unten: *Talking like a diplomat or politician.* Zusätzlicher Verweis auf die *UN strategies* (Aufgabe 5 **a)**, S. 35). Die Aufgabe kann auch als **Hausaufgabe** gestellt werden.

Lösungsvorschlag   *Keywords from the text (ll. 17–59): joint operations – deployment of forces – resolving the causes of a conflict – stepping up a political process – beginning negotiations – reconstruction and development – coordination of humanitarian efforts – adopting and implementing resolutions – developing strategies for peacekeeping/humanitarian work/human rights – etc.*

Research

5 Find out about Ban's personality and public image …

Verweis auf *Useful phrases* zu *Talking about images*. Die Aufgabe kann als Additum zur individuellen Förderung eingesetzt werden.

| | International peacekeeping An NGO at work | **4** |

Lösungsvorschlag *Ban's personality/public image: friendly, modest, competent, hard-working, quiet sense of humour but not very charismatic.*

Text production **6 [💻] *Writing a speech***

Lösungsvorschlag Individuelle Lösungen.

Erweiterung *Write the script of a TV interview with the present Secretary-General of the UN. Do some research on the UN homepage.*

Website | **An NGO at work** | **p. 38**

HINTERGRUNDINFO

Seeds of Peace *was founded in 1993. Its purpose is to strengthen future leaders from conflict regions, especially the Middle East, and work with them on skills that are necessary in order to create and maintain a peaceful environment in which coexistence of "enemies" is possible. Although the focus is on the conflict between Palestinians and Israelis, the network of Seeds of Peace includes over 3,500 young people from South Asia, Cyprus and the Balkans. The model program starts every year with the International camp in Maine in the summer and is followed by international youth conferences, regional workshops, educational and professional opportunities and adult educator programs – all dedicated to bringing forward the development of empathy, respect and confidence in the young*

people and teaching them the leadership, communication and negotiation skills they will need in the future. Every year there are more than 2,000 applicants who want to take part in the program. However, only 300 are selected by their governments according to the applicants' academic performance and leadership ability.

*The documentary **"Seeds of Peace"** (2004) gives an insight into the work of the organisation. Marjan Safinia and Joseph Boyle, both producer and director of the film, accompany participants in the Seeds of Peace program to the summer camp in Maine and show the young people's experiences in the process from being "enemies" to forming friendships.*

Lernwortschatz *NGO, independent, to address, emergency, to mobilise, contribution (to), to influence, to react, to adhere (to), diplomatic, message, to arouse, to participate (in), competency, to achieve, to provide*

Materialien → Online-Link: 601002-0016

Evaluation **1 *Looking at a homepage***

Evtl. **Hausaufgabe** zur Stunde mit Notizen, dann Besprechung im Kursgespräch mit Verweis auf *Useful phrases* zu *Talking about parts of a whole* und *Fact file* zu *NGO*. Eine lange Liste mit NGOs finden die S unter: http://csr-news.net/main/menue/menu_orga/orga/orga_ngos/.

Lösungsvorschlag a) *Clearly divided into five separate boxes in two rows: at the top box 1 (five head-and-shoulders pictures of a group of three young men and two young women of different ethnicity – all looking confidently and in a friendly manner – against a green background) and box 2 (name, logo and slogan of the NGO); below three boxes next to each other with a parallel build-up of photo plus statement – box 3 presents the beginning of a programmatic statement made by an NGO spokesperson, boxes 4 and 5 present quotations by two respected politicians (former US president Clinton, Palestinian president Abbas).*

b) *SoP plants the "seeds of peace" by working with young future leaders from Israel and Palestine for peaceful coexistence and mutual understanding. Its work is effective, successful and officially acknowledged. The colour green dominates the clearly structured layout and thus sends a message of hope of a better future in the Middle East.*

c) Individuelle S-Antworten.

65

4   International peacekeeping   An NGO at work

Erweiterung   Vorwissen der S zum *Middle East conflict* erfragen.

Research   **2 [🖥] *Conducting website research***

Bearbeitung entweder als **Hausaufgabe** oder über den Internetzugang der Schule. Die S präsentieren ihre Lösungen zu Aufgabe **a)** auf Folie (*talking in role as a representative of Seeds of Peace*). Aufgabe **b)** erfolgt im Kursgespräch. Bei Aufgabe **c)** gibt L sprachliche Hilfe zu *making comparisons: In contrast to …; Compared with …; In terms of … the website of … is more attractive/effective/appealing than …*

Lösungsvorschlag   **a)** **Founded:** *Foreign correspondent John Wallach founded SoP in 1993, bringing together 46 Israeli, Palestinian and Egyptian teenagers in a peace camp.*
Main aim: *To empower young leaders from regions of conflict with the leadership skills required to advance reconciliation and coexistence (focusing on the Middle East but including leaders from South Asia, Cyprus and the Balkans).*
Methods: *Building a leadership network (currently over 3,500 young people from several conflict regions).*
Main programmes: *Begin at the International Camp in Maine and continue with international youth conferences, regional workshops, educational and professional opportunities, and an adult educator program.*
Promotion of competencies/attitudes: *To develop empathy, respect, and confidence as well as leadership, communication and negotiation skills.*
"Seeds Store" products: *Bags, fragrance, tie, scarf, pin, bracelet, T-shirt.*
Skills of a volunteer: *computer, graphic design, Internet research, office work, fundraising, mass mailings, special events planning, public relations (check the online form for volunteer applications).*
"The Olive Branch": *Youth magazine of Seeds of Peace (available online; the title symbolises peace).*

b) *Very difficult, regions of conflict often suffer because of financial interests of different groups, for example: oil, diamonds and other resources. Important economic role for western world, Interests of big industrial nations and business companies. Therefore it is difficult to empower young leaders or leaders without any selfish financial interests. Success of Seeds of Peace must be doubted.*

c) *Boring and old fashioned. Bill Clinton does not attract the attention of young visitors to the website. It seems to be made for people who know Seeds of Peace. Not created like a website that tries to inform a great variety of people from different nations. Websites of Amnesty International and Greenpeace as boring as the one shown above.*
Conclusion: *Most of these websites are of good content, but of bad visual appearance.*

Evaluation   **3 [👥] *Find out more about NGOs***

Als Ausgangspunkt dient die *Fact file* zu *NGOs*. Eine erste Vertiefung erfolgt über die Eingabe des Stichworts *NGO* oder *non-governmental organisation* in Wikipedia (Unterpunkt: *Methods*). Von den S werden weitere Beispiele und Ziele genannt, z.B: *Greenpeace – protection of the environment; Amnesty International – helping political prisoners;* etc.

Lösungsvorschlag   ***Varying methods***
- *Acting as lobbyists to influence policy-making (i.e. public relations campaigns to mobilise public support and contributions for aid, lobbying with or consulting governments).*
- *Establishing links with community groups in developing countries.*
- *Conducting aid programmes (e.g. providing needy people with the equipment and skills to find food and clean drinking water).*

Assessing effectiveness
NGOs: short reaction time, no need to be diplomatic, may use unusual methods, etc.

66

International peacekeeping   The world today – spotlight on Africa   **4**

Government organisations: greater political, military and economic power; may exercise a greater influence through diplomacy, threats or interventions; etc.

Video clip   **4** [3 🎬] *Viewing a trailer*

Materialien   → Film, Track 3

[3 🎬]   Der *trailer* (*length: 4:46 min*) kann zur Vertiefung bzw. individuellen Förderung eingesetzt werden. **Track 3** wird als **Hausaufgabe** in Einzelarbeit auf der CD-ROM angeschaut.

Lösungsvorschlag   ***Information provided about Seeds of Peace in the trailer:*** *The trailer focuses on how peace is made between two opposing groups. It follows the events in a camp where 166 young Israelis and Palestinian met for 21 days to admit their hatred/to share arguments/to deal with their conflicts/to understand each other's perspectives and become friends. It shows the difficulty the moderator faced in a crisis situation and his method of overcoming this critical moment.*
References to the award-winning Seeds Documentary: *Through text on screen with (enthusiastic) audience reactions and comments from film reviews.*
Assessment of effectiveness: *May be related to the amount and usefulness of the information, the authenticity of the film material and the statements, the mostly dramatic music (calm at the end) and the focus on mutual hatred and emotional moments.*

Text production   **5** [🖵] *Writing an article*

L-Impulse: *For information on what happens in the camp in Maine or help with form and language, go to the Seeds of Peace website and check letters and articles from the online magazine "The Olive Branch". For ideas about the work of a volunteer in the New York office of Seeds of Peace, revise the skills of a volunteer collected in task 2* **a)**.

Erweiterung   Aufgabe 6 (S. 35): *Hot seat with a Palestinian and an Israeli representative.*

Cartoon | **The world today – spotlight on Africa** | **p. 39** |

HINTERGRUNDINFO

The African Union (AU) is the successor of the OAU, the Organisation of African Unity, that came into existence during the decolonisation struggles in the early 1960s. It was said, however, to be ineffective and was known as the "dictators' club". In 2002 all 53 states (except Morocco, which left the OAU in 1984) of the African continent formed the AU aiming for the unification of the continent, the strengthening of peace among African nations, the encouragement of democracy and good governance, and the enhancing of sustainable growth. In March 2004 a pan-African parliament was implemented that now functions as an advisor to the AU Heads of States and deals with continent-wide issues like AIDS/HIV, civil wars, poverty, famines and desertification and the spread of democracy. For the future the AU also plans to establish a human rights court, a central bank and a monetary fund. By 2023, it aims for a single currency and the creation of an African Economic Community. A current issue of the African Union is the voluntary "peer review" scheme, whose purpose is to keep an eye on democratic principles and sound economic practices to be applied in every member state. The working languages of the AU are: Arabic, English, French and Portuguese and, if possible, other African languages.

The African Union's structure is similar to that of the European Union. There are four principal organs:
1. The <u>Assembly</u>, the main decision-making body, in which the Heads of State or the governments' representatives are members.
2. The <u>Executive Council</u>, that is formed by the foreign ministers and advises the Assembly's members.
3. The <u>Commission</u>, which is a key organ and plays a central role within the AU, representing the organisation and defending its interests. The members are eight commissioners plus a Chairperson and a Deputy Chairperson. All of them hold individual portfolios, bring forward AU policies and coordinate the body's activities and meetings.

4 International peacekeeping   The world today – spotlight on Africa

4. The _Permanent Representatives' Committee_, which is responsible for the preparation of the Executive Council's work.

Aims and activities of NGOs active in Africa:
Human Rights Watch is the largest human rights organisation based in the United States. It was founded in 1988 and since then its aim has been the prevention of discrimination, the upholding of political freedom, the protection of people from inhumane conduct in wartime and bringing justice to the victims by taking offenders to court. The organisation investigates abuses in countries all over the world and publishes its results and findings in books or reports. Human Rights Watch also talks to government officials and people in responsible positions in order to urge changes and improve conditions. Human Rights Watch operates in all African countries. One of their current projects is the sufficient protection of girls and women in Darfur as in this war-torn country females are still not safe and suffer rape and brutal attacks committed by government forces and armed groups.

CARE was founded in 1945 and is a leading humanitarian organisation fighting poverty worldwide. Its focus is on poor women as it is often the mothers and wives who can change conditions for their families. The organisation works in over 66 countries worldwide aiming at the improvement of basic education, the prevention of the spread of Aids/HIV, the increase in access to clean water and sanitation, the expansion of economic opportunity and the protection of natural resources. In Ethiopia the SCOPE (Strengthening Communities through Partnerships for Education) project provides schools with useful material to improve learning processes and support teachers with information on crucial topics like HIV, nutrition and health.

Doctors without Borders (MSF/Médecins sans Frontières) is an international humanitarian aid organisation that was founded in 1971. Its major aim is to give emergency medical assistance to people in danger, especially those in developing countries and victims of natural or man-made disasters. In 1999 the organisation was awarded the Nobel Prize for its pioneering humanitarian work on all continents. MSF provides medical treatment for the poor by sending out volunteer doctors and nurses and offering free training for people living in third world countries. The organisation also conducts vaccination campaigns, supports water and sanitation improvement, feeds the poor, distributes drugs and medical supplies and offers Aids care and prevention.

Lernwortschatz	summit (meeting), to consist, unity, to secure, growth, market, currency, defence, drought, abuse, famine, poverty, dictatorship, civil war, warlord, caption, to convey, current, threatening, role
Materialien	→ Online-Link: 601002-0017
Discussion	Die drei _Fact files_ auf den Seiten 34–39 (_UN – NGO – African Union_) decken das wesentliche Bezugswissen für die Bearbeitung der Aufgaben zu dem Thema _The situation in Africa – problems, conflicts, positive things_ ab. Der Einstieg erfolgt über ein _Brainstorming: Have you ever been to Africa? What do you know about/associate with this continent?_ Positive und negative Assoziationen werden als Raster gegenübergestellt und an der Tafel festgehalten: _What is in the news at the moment? Would you like to visit an African country? Why?/Why not?_

Discussion

1 Talking about a cartoon

Bei Teilaufgabe **a)** verweist L vorab auf die _Useful phrases_ zu _Talking about negative feelings_. Die S ergänzen weitere Adjektive. Es folgt eine Minute Stillarbeit, danach S-Äußerungen dazu. Die Aufgaben **b)** und **c)** werden im Kursgespräch behandelt, **d)** zunächst in Einzel- oder Partnerarbeit, danach im Plenum.

Alternative   Die Aufgaben **a)** bis **d)** können als vorbereitende **Hausaufgabe** zu der Stunde gestellt werden, danach erfolgt die Besprechung im Plenum.

Lösungsvorschlag   **a)** Individuelle S-Äußerungen.

b) _Pictorial elements: 15 figures are sitting at a table which has the inscription "Africa" and is shaped like this continent; the participants of this meeting are uniformly dressed in black coats with hoods, their heads are skulls, some carry flags; there is no clearly recognizable chairperson, some are turned to a neighbour, some are looking straight ahead; nine of the figures have "names/problems" imprinted on their cloaks/coats._

| | International peacekeeping   The world today – spotlight on Africa | **4** |

c) **Message:** *The current situation in, and the prospects for Africa are gloomy/hopeless. The situation described is a meeting of the African Union, probably with the intention of discussing a problem or agreeing on closer political/economic unity/cooperation. The meeting claims to portray the reality of such a meeting: no leadership/unity – a continent with an overwhelming number of problems for which the single states themselves are mainly responsible – a common solution to these problems seems impossible – etc.*

d) *Child soldiers, prostitution, etc.*

Discussion

2 [𝄞] *Discussing priorities*

Zusatzmaterial

→ Kopiervorlage 8/8a (24 discussion strategies – card game)

Arbeitsteilige Gruppenarbeit zur Einschätzung der in Aufgabe 1 angesprochenen Probleme aus der Sicht der drei Perspektiven UN, NGO, AU. Möglich sind je zwei Gruppen mit 4–5 S. Es folgt ein Zwischenvergleich der beiden Gruppen mit gleicher Perspektive. Danach Vortrag der Ergebnisse (Folie/Poster) mit einem Vergleich der unterschiedlichen Blickwinkel und einer Begründung der Unterschiede unter Rückbezug auf den Cartoon.

Alternative

Aufgabe 4 kann zur Vorbereitung der NGO-Perspektive vorgezogen werden.

Lösungsvorschlag

Most pressing current problems
UN: warlord, dictatorship, civil war,
AU: drought, famine, disease,
Humanitarian NGO: rights abuses, poverty, hunger.

The cartoon paints a fair picture of African problems, as concerns from different points of view are reflected. The UN is concerned about different problems than a Humanitarian NGO and all these different sorrows are shown in the cartoon. On the other hand the cartoon paints a very depressing image of Africa. Modern Africa does not only consist of poverty, civil war and diseases, but also of great landscapes, an improving economic situation and a better relationship between black and white.

Erweiterung

• Eine Recherche zur aktuellen Lage Afrikas als **Hausaufgabe** ist vor der Beantwortung der letzten Fragestellung sinnvoll.
• Nach dieser Übung bietet sich der Einsatz von **Kopiervorlage 8/8a** (Seite 100/101) an. Die beiden Arbeitsblätter enthalten die Diskussionsstrategien von S. 55 (Themenheft) zum Ausschneiden und eine Spielanleitung für ein Kartenspiel zum Training dieser Strategien.

Research

3 *Researching a current conflict in Africa*

Recherche eines aktuellen afrikanischen Krisenherdes (Internet), entweder als Hausaufgabe oder S-Vortrag (individuelle Förderung).

Lösungsvorschlag

Example: Darfur (a region in Sudan which has been in a state of humanitarian emergency since 2003 due to an unusually long period of drought).
The conflicting parties: *the people of the largely nomadic, Arab-speaking north of Darfur are fighting against the non-Arabic speaking farmers in the south over natural resources (food and oil). The president of the country represents the interests of the north and has supported an Arab militia (the riding warriors of the Janjaweed) in their fight against the southern population, which is reported to include torture, rape, murder and deportation. Many people from Darfur have left their villages and fled to Chad. 300,000 people have died and five million people have been forced to leave their homes.*
Assessment: *Western media focus on the grave humanitarian crisis and Sudan's corrupt totalitarian regime. Other nations have special interests which prevent a unified international approach, e.g. China has been accused of supplying weapons and money to the Sudanese government, and India and Japan are important buyers of Sudanese oil.*

4 | International peacekeeping The USA – a global superpower

Role of the UN: UN forces are trying to send food by air, but the Janjaweed have often prevented and obstructed this aid with the silent support of the government. The UN are planning to take legal action against the president and top Sudanese leaders on genocide charges and crimes against humanity

Other options of solution: a Security Council resolution – pressure on the government (economic sanctions, import and export bans, …), militarily enforced delivery of aid; military action by African Union forces to topple the government; the deployment of UN troops, etc.

Report   **4 Giving a report: …**

L kann Stichpunkte vorgeben oder mit den S vereinbaren: *action areas – aim/purpose – programmes/projects – year of foundation – financial sources etc.* Die S konzentrieren sich auf NGOs mit englischen Namen, deren Arbeitsschwerpunkt unmittelbar erkennbar ist. Über gängige Suchmaschine kommt man zu *Directory of African NGOs:* http://www.unpan.org/NGO-Africa-Directory/index.htm. Die NGO-Profile sind geordnet nach *main action areas: agriculture, conflict resolution, education, environment, health, HIV/AIDS, micro-credit;* danach erst nach Ländern.

Lösungsvorschlag   African NGOs: Action Aid, World Vision, Women and development, Countryside Foundation for Sustainable Development, etc.

Visualising   **5 Three faces of Africa: …**

Ergänzung durch L: *Best destinations for tourists in Africa? Safest countries? Offers by travel agencies specialising in holidays in Africa?* Ggf. Hinweis auf die Website http://www.holidaysinafrica.co.za/.

Lösungsvorschlag   **Positive things Africa has to offer:** Colourful markets, wildlife safaris, cultural treasures (here: death mask of Tutankhamun's mummy, the popular icon for ancient Egypt at The Egyptian Museum; King Tutankhamun still rests in his intact tomb in the Valley of the Kings in a temperature-controlled glass case; discovery by Howard Carter in 1922.

Africa may be attractive to: Tourists interested in its culture/wildlife, exotic countries, adventure holidays, etc.

Combination of visuals   **The USA – a global superpower**   p. 40

HINTERGRUNDINFO

Uncle Sam: The first illustration of Uncle Sam, the national personification of the United States, dates back to 1852 and shows an obvious resemblance to President Andrew Jackson (1767–1845). The name "Uncle Sam" was used for the first time during the War of 1812. Common folklore holds that "Uncle Sam" can be traced back to the troops' meat supplier Samuel Wilson of Troy, New York. The soldiers, who received his food in barrels stamped "U.S.", referred to it as "Uncle Sam's". In 1961 the US Congress adopted the following resolution: "Resolved by the Senate and the House of Representatives that the Congress salutes Uncle Sam Wilson of Troy, New York, as the progenitor of America's National symbol of Uncle Sam." Over the centuries various pictures of Uncle Sam have been published. Furthermore, a comic with the same title and a short cartoon called "Uncle Sam's adventures" (1980s) has been printed.

September, 11, 2001: On the morning of September 11, 2001, the USA faced a series of coordinated suicide attacks. At about 9 am two hijacked airplanes hit the towers of the World Trade Centre (WTC) in Manhattan causing both buildings to collapse in the afternoon. Another airplane crashed into the Pentagon, the US military Headquarters, and severely damaged one side of it. The fourth plane, probably meant to attack the White House, crashed on a field near Pittsburgh/Pennsylvania. The attacks shock the American nation to its core and left people in fear and terror. About 3,000 people were killed, most of them civilians. The reactions to the 9/11 incidents were messages of condolence

International peacekeeping   The USA – a global superpower   4

from all over the world, coming to a climax in the French headline: "Nous sommes tous Américains." Most leaders of the Middle East countries, except Saddam Hussein (Iraq), condemned the attacks. However, there were also celebrations by Palestinians and people opposed to the US policy in Israel.

The 9/11 report hardened the US account that the organisation al-Qaeda with its head Osama bin Laden was responsible for the attacks based on several threats against Americans (fatwa) before 2001 and the strong animosity against US foreign policy. President George W. Bush addressed the nation promising to hunt down and punish those responsible. A coalition of international forces was created in order to remove the Taliban regime in Afghanistan, which was accused of harbouring al-Qaeda. The USA Patriot Act was also a consequence of 9/11 as were an increase in the arrest of terrorist suspects and the establishment of a detention centre at Guantanamo Bay, Cuba for "illegal enemy combatants". The American people responded with admiration for those who risked their lives to help in the disaster, especially fire-fighters, and patriotism. However, verbal abuse and hate crime against people from the Middle East also took place. Domestic security was an issue in other countries, too, and anti-terrorism legislation was introduced in several states worldwide. The "Global War on Terror", initiated by the President of the USA, resulted in an increase in military operations, economic measures and political pressures on suspects, especially in the US. In October 2001, the invasion of Afghanistan began. Its result was the removal of the Taliban regime. However, the al-Qaeda network could not be destroyed and is also held responsible for the terrorist attacks in Madrid and London.

Lernwortschatz	personification, to fight back, democracy, superpower, global policeman, leader, ambassador, imperial, defender
Materialien	→ Online-Link: 601002-0018
Discussion	Kurzer Rückbezug auf *global hot spots today* (S. 34, Aufgaben 4 und 5 **a)**) als Einstieg in das Thema *The global roles of the USA and the events on September, 11, 2001*. Mögliche L-Impulse: *What role does the USA play in these conflicts? If its role is an active one, what strategy does it pursue?*

Describing a picture	## 1 Describe Uncle Sam.
	Bei den Aufgaben 1 und 2 sollte auf eine klare Differenzierung zwischen *description* und *analysis* geachtet werden.
Alternative	Die Aufgaben 1–3 sind als zusammenfassende **Hausaufgabe** möglich.
Lösungsvorschlag	**Parallels:** Old gentleman, white beard, white curly hair, clothes (hat, tie, jacket, trousers) with the stars/stripes/colours of the American flag.

Differences
- In the colour (mainly red/white/blue vs. black and white).
- In the representation (upper half of the body vs. full figure).
- In the posture (sitting vs. standing, looking at the viewer vs. sideways position).
- In the facial expression (determined/aggressive/benevolent).
- In the gesture (pointing a finger vs. holding a red knife vs. feeding with a spoon).

Analysis	## 2 In what situations is Uncle Sam depicted?
	Verweis auf *Useful phrases* zu *Global roles*. Evtl. arbeitsteiliges Vorgehen in Partnerarbeit. Kollokationsfeld: *crucial, dominant, key, leading, prominent, significant role, minor, subordinate, passive role, etc.* Die Ergebnissicherung erfolgt in einem Raster an der Tafel.
Lösungsvorschlag	**Poster:** Uncle Sam is looking for new army recruits/volunteers. **No global role** is reflected here. The area of deployment may be at home for self-defense or abroad in international operations. The professional US army needs volunteers who ideally should join to serve their country in a patriotic spirit.

71

4 International peacekeeping   The USA – a global superpower

Cartoon 1: Uncle Sam is standing with outstretched legs, a bloody knife in his right hand and one half of the globe in his left hand – his posture is triumphant, proud and self-confident. The other half of the globe has fallen to the ground and "flattened" a (probably dead) victim whose figure is barely recognizable. *Global role:* The USA as an imperial power, employing its military power for clearly imperialist purposes.

Cartoon 2: Uncle Sam is sitting on a ridiculously small chair opposite a fragile "world figure" with a globe as its head. Uncle Sam is offering the "food of democracy" to the starving figure, who is bent forward and examining the offer with an expressionless face. *Global role:* The USA as the prosperous benefactor who advocates democracy as a remedy to a suffering world which urgently needs help = ambassador of democracy.

Discussion

3 Where would you expect to find similar cartoons today? Explain.

Erweiternde Fragestellung: *As an editor of the newspaper …, would you print these two cartoons? Why?/Why not?*

Lösungsvorschlag

Poster: Clearly historic poster although Uncle Sam is still an accepted and instantly recognised figure in the media. Today, the well known posture and slogan of this poster are often used in non-military contexts in adapted form for advertising a product or criticism of the USA.

Cartoon 1: A cartoon of this blatant style and with this clearly anti-American sentiment and message may today be found in countries which see the USA as an aggressive force which tries to spread its materialist values all over the world through its military power, thus enlarging its area of control and influence at all costs.

Cartoon 2: A cartoon which is critical of the US attempt to offer democracy as a global remedy for the developing countries may be found all over the world, even in Europe or the USA itself.

Describing a photo

4 Describe the photo taken on September 11, 2001.

Mögliche Erweiterung: *Find other photos of the same historic event. How do they differ from this one?*

Lösungsvorschlag

a) Taken from a considerable distance on September 11, 2001 – possibly from a ship – the photo shows Manhattan with its skyscraper-lined skyline from a distance. The burning Twin Towers on the left and the sunlit Statue of Liberty, which in this picture seems to be a part of Manhattan but in reality stands on a small separate island, are the two most prominent elements of the photo and form a significant contrast. The once impressive Manhattan skyline is sandwiched between the water in the foreground and the massive clouds in the sky.

b) **Possible symbolic meanings/undertones:** threat to democracy; the World Trade Center under attack (as symbol of America's economic power); American society and values remain unhurt and will survive; the impact of terrorism; etc.

Research

5 What exactly happened on September 11, 2001?

Mögliche vertiefende **Hausaufgabe.**

Lösungsvorschlag

a) See Hintergrundinfo on the events on September 11, 2001 on p. 70.

b) **Possible captions from different perspectives**
- The American perspective: Manhattan under attack/Terrorism hits America's heart.
- The European perspective: Attack on the western world. Who will be the next to be struck by terrorism?
- The Muslim fundamentalist perspective: Declaration of war on America. We will strike again …

Erweiterung

Schriftliche Zusammenfassung der Ergebnisse: *Compare the four visuals on this page and relate them to the global roles of the USA in the past and in the present.*

International peacekeeping Courtesy of the red, white and blue 4

Video clip   **6 [🖥] *Viewing a docu-clip on the Internet: ...***

Lernwortschatz   *victim, gruesome, grief, terrorism, granted, intimidating, to evolve, reign, to weed out, assassination, hijacking, hostage, rescue, exile, embassy, to release, campaign, responsibility, to convict, to replace (sth by sth else), to avenge, suicide, to deny*

CD-ROM   Die Dokumentation stammt aus dem Jahre 2003 (*length: 06:26, Open Source Video, USA government film*). Die Dokumenten-CD-ROM enthält ein PDF mit dem Transkript des Videoclips. Die S schauen die Dokumentation entweder als **Hausaufgabe** oder sie wird zweimal im Unterricht angeschaut. Alternativ folgt zu den Aufgabenstellungen **a)** bis **c)** entweder eine *class discussion* oder eine Bearbeitung als *written comment* or talk.

Lösungsvorschlag   a) *Information on 9/11*
   - *In the introduction: a shocking event – Americans as victims of an attack previously seen as impossible – reactions: horror and grief.*
   - *In the chronological description of major historical terror attacks: 9/11 as the deadliest terrorist attack in history – planned by Osama bin Laden's al-Qaeda – four passenger jets were hijacked – two crashed into the World Trade Centre, one crashed into the Pentagon and one came down in rural Pennsylvania – thousands of lives were lost – innocent citizens of more than 80 nations were killed.*
   - *Possible open questions: the exact number of terrorists and victims – the significance of the targets – the intention behind the attack – responses and reactions – etc.*

   b) ***Audio-visual means:*** *authentic film material (focus on victims) – personal statements – voiceover – dramatic music – maps to show locations – etc.*
   Sections: *introduction to the topic – definitions of terrorism – origin/history of terrorism – terrorist tactics today – places touched by terrorism (examples) – 9/11 as the deadliest example – statements – conclusion (with open question to the viewer).*
   Objectivity: *clearly western viewpoint, fairly objective contextualisation of 9/11.*

   c) Individuelle Antworten.

Erweiterung   *Write a review and send it to the site. Search the site for other docu-clips on terrorism. Compare them with the given one in terms of information, audio-visual means, structure and objectivity.*

Protest song   **[₇◎] Courtesy of the red, white and blue**   p. 41

HINTERGRUNDINFO

The flag of the USA: *The colours red, white and blue refer to the flag of the USA, also known as "Stars and Stripes" or "Old Glory". The 13 red stripes refer to the colonies that once were the first states of the Union while the 50 stars stand for the fifty states of the US today. Worldwide the flag is not only shown to refer to the US but also to its ideology and set of ideas including freedom and the rights guaranteed in the US Constitution.*

The Fourth of July, *also called "Independence Day", is a federal holiday in the US on which fireworks, parades, barbecues and picnics take place to commemorate the adoption of the Declaration of Independence in 1776 and celebrate the history, government and the traditions of the USA. Decorations in the colours red, white and blue can be found everywhere and patriotic songs and the national anthem are popular music on that day.*

The Statue of Liberty, *originally called "Liberty Enlightening the World", was given to the USA by France as a present for the celebration of the US's centennial. Given as a gesture of friendship, the statue, made by the sculptor Frédéric Auguste Bartholdi, is today located on Liberty Island/New York welcoming everyone coming to the USA. Like the American flag the statue represents liberty and the escape from oppression. The seven spikes of its crown stand for the seven seas and seven continents while the torch represents enlightenment.*

American Country music *originates in the Southern United States and the Appalachian Mountains. It has its roots in traditional folk music, Celtic music, blues and gospel. The term spread in the 1940s and was widely used in the 1970s. However, countrymusic already evolved in the 1920s. Country music is still*

73

4 | International peacekeeping — Courtesy of the red, white and blue

very popular and had one of its best years (regarding album sales) in 2006. One of the top-selling country artists of all time is Garth Brooks.

Toby Keith was born in Oklahoma in 1961. Before becoming a professional singer and songwriter, he worked for the oil industry. His first album "Toby Keith" was a great success in 1993, as were his following 15 albums. He has won several awards for his music. His album "Unleashed", which was released in 2002, has been controversial, especially because of the song "Courtesy of the Red, White and Blue (the angry American)".

Lernwortschatz	to stand up, to recognise, to serve, flag, battle
Materialien	→ CD, Track 7 • Online-Link: 601002-0019
Discussion	Kurz-Wiederholung: *Uncle Sam – the Statue of Liberty – the events on 9/11.* Vorwissen abrufen: *the American flag – American country music.* Erwartung aufbauen *(a patriotic response to the events on September 11, 2001)*: We are going to deal with a song called "Courtesy of the red, white and blue" (courtesy of = with the official permission of/acting on behalf of; red/white/blue = colours of the American flag). What do you expect the lyrics and music to be like?

Comprehension

1 *Read the lyrics and look at the photo of Toby Keith.*

Mögliche vorbereitende **Hausaufgabe** (auch zusammen mit Aufgabe 2). Die Ergebnisse werden in einem Tafelbild (drei Spalten, darunter das Resümee) festgehalten. Danach hören die S zweimal **Track 7** auf der CD-ROM.

[7⊚]

Lösungsvorschlag

The singer	His message	His photo
Basic information: American man – grew up in a patriotic family – loves his country; values: peace, freedom, justice.	He addresses the American people and sends a message of revenge to those responsible for the 9/11 attacks.	Casually dressed (cowboy hat, T-shirt) – guitar with the flag of the USA/the Stars and Stripes printed on it.

Summary: Toby Keith presents himself as an American patriot.

Analysis

2 *Analyse the American self-image as presented in this song.*

Vorbereitung: Detailliertes Lesen in Einzelarbeit mit Notieren von Schlüsselstellen und Kommentaren. Danach Austausch und wechselseitige Ergänzung in Partnerarbeit. Die Ergebnissicherung im Kursgespräch an der Tafel. Alternativ ist die schriftliche Zusammenfassung der Ergebnisse als **Hausaufgabe** denkbar.

Lösungsvorschlag

The American self-image (the singer speaks as "we", thus claiming to represent America as a whole): strong patriotism – the army as a necessary tool to defend the country – casualties have to be accepted/sacrifices are necessary to defend the American way of life – strong support for family unity and values – the USA as a strong country which is able to take revenge/to retaliate militarily.

Imagery: Personifications of America: Uncle Sam and Mother Freedom (= the figure at the top of the Statue of Liberty).
Symbols of America: the bald-headed eagle, the Statue of Liberty, the flag.
Symbolic actions: having a big black eye = severe wound or injury; shaking one's fist = expressing rage and promising revenge; the eagle will fly = air force attacks; ringing her bell = giving a warning and calling to action; raining down on you = exposed to the full force of (bomb) attacks; rattling his cage = provocation, challenge.
Metaphor: the big dog = the superpower USA.

Historical allusions: to the dead of previous wars/victories (ll. 2–7), the attacks of 9/11 (ll. 16–19),

the wars in Afghanistan and Iraq as a response to 9/11 (ll. 20–23),
America as the no. 1 enemy (ll. 25–26),
call to action to defend freedom (ll. 31–32).

Photo of the burning Twin Towers: Suitable only as part of the booklet. Needs to be
complemented by other visuals expressing America's patriotism and military response.

Listening

3 *What do you expect the music to be like?*

[7◉] Verweis auf *Useful phrases* zu *Talking about songs*. Die S fixieren ihre Erwartungen schriftlich
für einen späteren Rückbezug und Vergleich nach dem Hören. Die Aussagen werden
textbezogen begründet, danach Überprüfung mit der Aufnahme des *Songs*.

Lösungsvorschlag Individuelle Einschätzungen.

Discussion

4 *Why do you think the song went down well ...*

Lösungsvorschlag *The clear message, language (colloquialisms and slang expressions in the lyrics) and emotions
(aggressive, belligerent, threatening, etc.) perfectly hit the public post-9/11 mood in the USA
(strong sense of national unity, unquestioning support for military action, call for revenge,
feeling of threat).*

Mood and self-image now: *Patriotism (2001–2003) turned into disillusionment with the war on
terrorism especially in Iraq in President Bush's second term of office in the White House (2005–
2008). The charisma and leadership of the new American President and the success of his
policies in dealing with the economic problems at home and the management of international
interventions (Iraq/Afghanistan) will determine America's mood and self-image: depressed/
self-critical/disillusioned/pessimistic vs. hopeful/active/optimistic/single-handed actions vs.
global cooperation with its allies and the UN.*

Erweiterung Hinführung zum Videoclip zum Aufbau einer Erwartungshaltung: *What are your ideas for a
video clip? Would you prefer a "performance clip" (i.e. the singer performing the song live on
stage) or a "concept clip" (i.e. a clip in which the singer does not appear; instead, pictures
illustrate the lyrics and the mood of the song)?*

Comprehension

5 [🖳] *Watch the music video versions of this song ...*

Die S schauen das offizielle Video (*Dreamworks Records 2002; length: 03:27 min*) zweimal an. L
überprüft das Grob- und Detailverstehen und schließt die Frage an: *What does the official clip
not show? Why not?* Mögliche Antwort: *The official clip does not contain (refer back to the
expectations in the optional pre-viewing task) pictures of Uncle Sam, the events of 9/11 and war
victims/casualties*. Als **Hausaufgabe** analysieren die S weitere Versionen.

Lösungsvorschlag **Official video:** *Mix of performance and concept clip: American flag at the beginning and ending
= frame; Toby Keith on a stage (full/medium shots and close-ups of his face) with many US flags
as a backdrop and a cheering, enthusiastic audience; childhood family photos (ll. 8–15);
authentic footage (film material) of soldiers, tanks, helicopters in action and Toby Keith visiting
and performing for soldiers at war (here: Iraq); static shots of the Statue of Liberty and a
certificate given to the singer in recognition of his support for the troops.*

Other video versions: *Usually concept clips in the form of a series of photos illustrating the lyrics
(for copyright reasons no photos of the singer performing live).*

Erweiterung **Post-viewing activities**
- **Kommentierung:** *The video clip has the sub-title "The Angry American". To what extent does
this phrase fit the clip?*

75

4 International peacekeeping America's role in the world: four options

- **Leseverstehen:** *Read the Internet comments on the clip. Are the responses generally favourable or rather critical? Who has written these comments?*
- **Schreiben:**
  1. *Write your own comment on the official video clip and post it to the site for publication.*
  2. *Write a personal letter to Toby Keith in response to this video clip.*
  3. *Write the script of an interview with the singer in which he looks back on this song and his visits to the troops in Iraq from a present-day perspective.*

Education programme

America's role in the world: four options
p. 42

HINTERGRUNDINFO

Saddam Hussein, *once the best known and most hated Arab leader, was born in 1937 in a village near Tikrit/Iraq. He went to college in Baghdad, where he joined the Baath party at the age of 20. The Arab Socialist Baath party, which is its full name, was founded in Syria in the 1940s. Baathism in Iraq, where the party was established in 1951, is associated with radical Arab nationalism. In 1958, the British-installed Iraqi monarchy was overthrown and five years later, which Saddam Hussein spent in exile as he had to flee Iraq after being accused of a conspiracy against the prime minister, the Baath party came into power and Saddam returned to Baghdad. Together with General Ahmad Hasan al-Bakr he led the party and was able to increase his power until he was made Head of State in 1979. Saddam was determined to remain leader of Iraq as long as possible and as his first action as President he killed all his rivals. His leadership style as dictator, which he claimed was necessary for the good of the nation's unity, meant terror to the Iraqis and especially his opponents whom he arrested and executed. He also did not hesitate to use chemical weapons against the Kurds. In 1980 he led a war against Iran, which ended in a ceasefire but was propagated by Saddam as a victory for Iraq. Ten years later he started the second Gulf War invading the neighbouring country, Kuwait, to plunder her oil.*

In 2003, the US army invaded Iraq and Saddam Hussein was captured by the US forces. He was brought to trial by the Iraqi interim government that had been installed by the US forces and was convicted and executed in 2006.

The Mount Rushmore National Memorial *in Keystone/South Dakota is one of America's historic places visited by more than two million people annually. The former name of Mount Rushmore, which was named after a popular New York lawyer in 1885, was Lakota Sioux as the territory once belonged to the Lakota tribe. The memorial shows the heads of four former US presidents: George Washington (1732–1799), Thomas Jefferson (1743–1826), Theodore Roosevelt (1858–1919) and Abraham Lincoln (1809–1865), who represent 150 years of US history and where chosen by the sculptor Gutzon Borglum because of their endeavors to preserve the Republic and expand its territory. The aim of the project, which started in 1927 and was finished in 1941, was to make the area of the Black Hills more attractive to tourists. There is also a chamber cut into the rock, in which the text of the Declaration of Independence and the Constitution, biographies of the four presidents and Borglum, and the history of the US can be found.*

Lernwortschatz *values, to measure, to keep in check, to intervene (in), to pressure (AE), to spark, to reject, deep-seated, access (to), vital, to be at stake, interdependent, to take the initiative, sovereignty, ally, involvement (in), a sagging economy, decaying, shaky*

Materialien → Online-Link: 601002-0020

Discussion Einstieg in das Thema *Options for America's global role – and their pros and cons* über L-Impuls: *In your opinion, should the USA focus on protecting its homeland or rather actively take on a global role? If the USA acts as a global power, what aims should it pursue?*

Discussion **1 Describe the pictures and discuss the extent ...**

Lösungsvorschlag *Pictures numbered from top to bottom*
1. *Two US soldiers on a ladder have covered a gigantic statue of Saddam Hussein with the American flag (sign of victory and conquest); they are obviously preparing to tear it down*

International peacekeeping   America's role in the world: four options   4

(from its pedestal?) with the help of a rope. **Policy option:** *Option 1 is the best choice because the USA toppled this tyrant in Iraq with the clear intention/promise to build democracy there.*

2. *Two armed American soldiers on patrol in foreign territory – one is checking a young boy, the second one is observing the surroundings with his machine-gun at the ready.* **Policy option:** *Option 2 is the best choice: the soldiers are likely to act abroad but it remains unclear what their task/mission/interest is.*

3. *Four young people (two of each sex, all dressed in grey trousers and white T-shirts) are standing close together and with physical contact in front of an oversized American flag. Two of them are white, one is black and one of them is of Asian origin. They are smiling and obviously happy to express their allegiance to the USA.* **Policy option:** *Option 3 is the option best illustrated by this picture if we assume that the four characters come from different countries (likewise, all four could be Americans).*

4. *Mount Rushmore as seen from a bird's eye perspective with two fighter jets in the foreground.* **Policy option:** *Option 4 is well represented here provided the fighter jets are American planes and on a defensive mission*

Text production   **2 [👥👥👥] *In groups, think of supporting arguments ...***

Arbeitsteilige Erarbeitung: Anwendung in Interviews mit Vertretern unterschiedlicher Organisationen oder Ländern, in Form einer politischen Rede eines amerikanischen Politikers oder in Form einer Podiumsdiskussion.

Lösungsvorschlag   a) *Supporting arguments and concerns*
Option 1 (spreading democracy)
Pros: *The United States is the best model for democracy; new democracies need military/ economic support in order to survive; the world depends on the USA as the only remaining superpower with a strong military to maintain peace and order and to support the principles of democracy, free markets, and freedom in the world; states in the hands of cruel and undemo-cratic leaders who terrorise their own people often threaten their neighbours and breed unrest around the world; such tyrants pose a danger to global peace and security; no other nation or the United Nations can be counted on to deal with these threats; as World War II showed, tyrants must be confronted and democracy implemented, otherwise the costs will be enormous.*
Cons: *There is no justification for interfering in another country's internal affairs; other political systems should be respected; democracy should never be enforced but evolve gradually in a nation; the US is not a credible leader of democracy abroad; you can't force other nations to establish democracies; etc.*

Option 2 (protecting US interests)
Pros: *In a dangerously unstable world with global terrorism and economic competition, there is no room for idealism; it is necessary to engage with the world pragmatically and selectively in order to promote US interests; US interests often require friendly relations with undemocratic governments; etc.*
Cons: *Acting without regard for other nations' interests and concerns will only lead to resentment, risk international violence and undermine international cooperation on critical global issues; relationships with dictators endanger the worldwide movement towards democracy; intervening only where self-interests are at stake could mean the acceptance of genocide and ethnic cleansing; etc.*

Option 3 (building a cooperative world)
Pros: *Global problems like environmental pollution, financial crises, refugees, deadly epidemics, AIDS and nuclear proliferation require international cooperation; only the USA has the power and influence to bring the nations of the world together; if the US acts in cooperation with NATO, the European Union or the UN, its actions are less open to criticism; unilateral actions will only increase anti-American feelings; etc.*
Cons: *Handing over power to international institutions means the loss of international influence; American values are in conflict with those of large parts of the world, therefore*

77

4 International peacekeeping Spot on facts: America's global role

cooperation not only won't work but it could even be dangerous; the USA can no longer respond flexibly and quickly to international challenges; etc.

Option 4 (protecting the US homeland)
Pros: *9/11 has shown that the USA is vulnerable, therefore security at home is a top priority; the United States has wasted a lot of money on supporting its allies and the developing countries: now it should concentrate on the threats at home; global initiatives have often only bred resentment and made new enemies; military spending should be limited to the defence of the US homeland, as a nation's first responsibility is to defend its citizens from harm; the US must try not to become involved in conflicts abroad; etc.*
Cons: *Pretending that the fate of the rest of the world matters little is foolish and dangerous; in its own self-interest, the US must use its influence and power to promote democracy and human rights in the world; the US homeland is best protected through a wise foreign policy based on the cooperation with allies and the UN; many countries in the world need the economic support of the US; etc.*

b) Individuelle und aktuelle Antworten.

Fact page

Spot on facts: America's global role p. 43

HINTERGRUNDINFO

The Monroe Doctrine *was issued as a Presidential doctrine in 1823. It strengthened the independence of the USA by stating that European powers were no longer to colonise or interfere with the affairs of the US and every attempt to do so would be regarded as a threat. The US on the other hand would stay neutral regarding any wars between Europe and its colonies. The doctrine got its name from US President James Monroe (1817–1825). A doctrine (lat. doctrina) is a code of beliefs or a system of statements often meant to be universal.*

Pearl Harbour, *a US navy base and the Headquarters of the US Pacific Fleet, is located on Hawaii and is associated with the attack by the Japanese navy on December 7, 1941. As Japan had not declared war on the USA, the attack came as a surprise and killed more than 2,300 people. It was meant as a preventive action in order to destroy the US Pacific Fleet and resulted in the engagement of the USA in World War II.*

Establishment of the United Nations: *The first step towards an international organisation was made during the Second World War in 1941, when the "Inter-Allied Declaration" was signed by those states fighting Nazi Germany. The "Atlantic Charter" of the same year, consisting of a proposal by Roosevelt and*

Churchill on a set of principals, was signed in Washington D.C. in 1942 by the allies. In this "Declaration by the United Nations" the term 'United Nations', which was created by US President Franklin D. Roosevelt, was first used. The affirmation and reaffirmation of the establishment of an early international organisation by the Soviet Union, the United Kingdom, the United States and China followed in the conferences of Moscow and Teheran in 1943. The same nations agreed on the structure, functioning and aims of this global organisation during the "Dumbarton Oaks Conference" in Washington D.C. in 1944. Finally, a declaration made by Roosevelt, Churchill and Stalin, in which they confirmed their aim to establish an international organisation in order to maintain peace and security in the world, followed and in the same year, 1945, representatives of 50 nations signed the UN Charter containing 111 articles in San Francisco.

The Truman Doctrine *is important regarding the beginning of the Cold War since it encourages those countries resisting communism and assures that the USA will support them in their resistance. It was proclaimed on March 12, 1947 by US President Harry S. Truman and aims to stop communism from spreading.*

Lernwortschatz *marked, unique, expansion, to interfere (in/with), involved (in), step, to occupy, attack, to withdraw, to shape, defender, evil, era, effort, to maintain, arms race, establishment, to avoid, recovery, collapse, to declare war on sb/sth, terrorism, unstable, mix*

International peacekeeping   Spot on facts: America's global role

4

Comprehension   **1 Which of the four global policy opitions (see previous page)...**

Den Einstieg in das Thema *America's global role from a historical perspective* bildet eine Kurzwiederholung der vier Handlungsoptionen (Themenheft, S. 42). Es folgt *scanning* der *Fact page* nach historischen Beispielen für die vier globalen Handlungsoptionen.

Erweiterung   *Why is it difficult to connect a) the Truman Doctrine (1947) and Cold War period, b) the 1990s and the beginning of the 21st century with one option only?*

Lösungsvorschlag   *Option 1 (promoting democracy): Period before and after the Declaration of Independence in 1776 – American Revolutionary War/American War of Independence against political oppression and the monarchy from 1775 to 1783 – fight for the right to self-determination and a federal democracy based on the core values of equality and freedom. World War II – US military intervention to secure the survival of democracy in Europe (1941); in the post-war years it helped build democracy in Germany.*

Option 2 (pursuing one's self-interest): Occupation of Hawaii and the Philippines in 1899 as the beginning of US imperialism in the first two decades of the 20th century.

Option 3 (building a cooperative world): In the post World War II period the USA cooperated with the west-European countries to build friendship; in 1945, it also supported the establishment of the United Nations.

Option 4 (protection of the US homeland): Policy of isolationism after the Monroe Doctrine (1823) – historically necessary to focus on the conquest of the continent and the stabilisation of the new country (until the closure of the frontier in 1890). Another period of isolationism in the 1920s and 1930s (The Roaring/Golden Twenties = a period of prosperity in the USA, followed by an economic depression in the 1930s after the stock market crash in 1929).

Analysis   **2 Compare and contrast the role of the UN ...**

Vergleichszeitraum ist 1945 bis heute.

Lösungsvorschlag

Global player: United Nations	Global player: USA
global organisation	most powerful country/military superpower
focus on peacemaking, human rights and economic development	focus on military/economic/political self-interest (e.g. its access to oil, the spread of democracy, the expansion of NATO)
generally respected, but often criticised for its ineffectiveness	countries differ in their opinions of the USA (cf. p. 44)
limited budget; dependent on the contributions of the member states	high defense budget
long reaction time: need for unity and consensus as a basis of joint action	short reaction time in a crisis: prepared to act single-handedly

Text production   **3 Write either a political keynote speech or an open letter of advice ...**

Aufgabe kann als **Hausaufgabe** gestellt werden. Dabei erfolgt ein Rückbezug auf *9/11 and global terrorism (p. 40)*, *America's four global options (p. 42)*, *Fact page "America's global roles" (p. 43)* und auf die Ergebnisse von Aufgabe 2 *(UN vs. USA)*.

Lösungsvorschlag   Individuelle Lösungen.

4 | International peacekeeping The opinion of the USA abroad

Statistics	**The opinion of the USA abroad**	**p. 44**

HINTERGRUNDINFO

The Pew Global Attitudes Project *is a series of public opinion surveys from all over the world. It claims to be unique, comprehensive and internationally comparable and offers its results to journalists, academics, policymakers and the public. The Project's aim is to examine attitudes towards key issues like globalisation, trade, democracy, terrorism and the view of the United States in the world.*

For information on **9/11:** *see* **Hintergrundinfo** *on p. 70/71.*

President Bush/War on terrorism: *George Walker Bush (born 1946) was the forty-third President of the USA and served two terms from January 2001 to January 2009. After the events of 9/11 Bush decided*

to invade Afghanistan and in October 2001 started a global War on Terrorism to overthrow the Taliban, to destroy al-Qaeda, and to capture Osama bin Laden. After his re-election in November 2004, Bush received increasing criticism at home and abroad. During his two terms he has had both the highest and the lowest domestic Gallup poll approval ratings of American Presidents with 90% after 9/11 down to less than 30% in 2008. Internationally, President Bush was criticised by the global anti-war and anti-globalisation campaigns for his foreign policy and especially his war in Iraq. His successor is confronted with expectations of an immediate pullout or at least a step-by-step withdrawal from Iraq.

Lernwortschatz — concerned (about/with), to view, attitude, US-led, poll, motive, to dominate, to target, to protect (sb from sth), statistics (pl), update, minority, majority, roughly, percentage, gradually, continually, sharply

Materialien — → Online-Link: 601002-0021

Comprehension — ### 1 *Compare the opinions of the US as a country ...*

Es geht um das Beschreiben und Bewerten absoluter Zahlen zum Thema *America's image in the world.* Die S ziehen Vergleiche innerhalb einer Zeile/Spalte oder zwischen zwei Zeilen/Spalten/Tabellen. Vorab das historische Hintergrundwissen zu *9/11* wiederholen und dabei unterscheiden zwischen *before* und *after 9/11.* Verweis auf *Useful phrases* zu *Describing statistical figures* und ihre Verwendung einfordern. Input für schwächere S zur Wiederholung: *making comparisons (in contrast to ..., compared with ...), describing a table (figures/numbers, lines and columns, etc.).*

Erweiterung — *How do the figures for Germany compare with those of other countries? What is striking about the figures for Spain?*

Lösungsvorschlag

Opinions of the ...	US as a country	Americans
General trends	Before 9/11: Positive image in Western Europe, Indonesia, Japan; negative image in Pakistan. In 2006: A noticeable deterioration of the approval figures in almost all countries except Russia and Pakistan. Now Japan, Great Britain, India and China are top of the list.	After 9/11 (2002): Positive image in all countries except Jordan and Turkey. In 2006: Best image in Western European countries, negative image in Turkey and Jordan.
Changes in a country between 2002 and 2006	Strong deterioration: Germany, Indonesia, Turkey. Slight deterioration: Japan. Modest improvement: Russia, Pakistan.	Declining figures in Western Europe, Russia, Indonesia and Turkey. Improving figures in Jordan, Japan and India.

80

Opinions of the ...	US as a country	Americans
Differences between nations in a given year.	_In 2002:_ Most favourable image in Great Britain, followed by Japan, France, Germany and Indonesia. _In 2003:_ Still the best image in the UK with the European countries following at a considerable distance and very low figures outside of Europe.	_In 2003:_ Great Britain has by far the best opinion with Russia in second place (very low rating in Indonesia). _In 2005:_ India and Great Britain have the highest figures, Jordan and Turkey the lowest.

Erweiterung

Further discussion: Why has the US war on terrorism, and especially the war in Iraq, been so severely criticised? Points of criticism: The war on terrorism ...
- is not based on a generally accepted definition of "terrorism" (one state's "terrorist" is another state's "freedom fighter"),
- is open-ended/indefinite because victory is impossible,
- is counterproductive because it supports terrorist recruitment/increases the likelihood of revenge attackas on the USA/radicalises a disillusioned youth in the Middle East,
- reveals double standards because the US is more lenient/understanding with regimes of geostrategic importance (e.g. Pakistan, Israel).

Analysis

2 To what extent do the three statistics support the view ...

Lösungsvorschlag

As a general global trend, the three statistics point out a deterioration in America's global image until 2007. This decline, however, cannot be proven for all countries and varies in its degree of deterioration from country to country. The basis for this global perception are largely President Bush's foreign policy and especially the US-led invasion of Iraq, which are obviously viewed as ineffective and unfounded. The global image of the US may experience a significant improvement with Bush's successor in office.

Research

3 [🖥] Check the Pew Global Attitudes Project for an update ...

Lösungsvorschlag

Individuelle Lösungen.

Editorial

Germany's army
p. 45

HINTERGRUNDINFO

The German army: From 1955 to October 1990, Germany's federal defence forces (Bundeswehr) was composed of the Army, the Navy and the Air Force. In October 1990, upon the reunification of Germany, the East German army was integrated into the now unified force.

The German army abroad: According to the German Basic Law, the role of the Bundeswehr is defensive only and before 1990 was strictly limited to support operations after natural disasters. Since a ruling of the Federal Constitutional Court in 1994, "defence" not only includes the protection of the borders of Germany, but also – if related to Germany's security – crisis reaction and conflict prevention anywhere in the world. Thus the German army may take part in

operations outside of the borders of Germany, as part of NATO or the EU and with a UN mandate. In 2008, for example, German forces were employed in considerable numbers in Afghanistan (ca. 3,600), Kosovo (ca. 2,200) and off the coast of Lebanon (ca. 830), but not in Iraq. Their main areas of responsibility are reconnaissance, medical aid, safeguarding, training and support in re-building the infrastructure.

Trouble spots Iraq and Afghanistan: In 2008, Afghanistan was increasingly perceived as failed state due to increasing Taliban violence (e.g. suicide and fire attacks), growing drug production and fragile State institutions. The campaign in Afghanistan successfully toppled the Taliban

4 | International peacekeeping Germany's army

regime, but has been significantly less successful in achieving the primary policy goal of stabilising the country and building a democratic Afghanistan in which al-Qaeda can no longer operate. Although foreign and Afghan troops have constrained repeated Taliban offensives, there has been a steady escalation in violence since NATO took charge of the Afghanistan mission in 2006 (roadside bombs, open attacks, etc.). In contrast to the deteriorating situation in Afghanistan, a 2007 American troop surge has been reported as successful in reducing violence in Iraq. At the same time, there is increasing pressure on the Iraqi government to develop the nation's security forces and the reconciliation of sectarian groups. In 2008, the overwhelming majority of Americans saw the invasion of Iraq as a costly mistake. The contenders for the presidency differed in their views on troop reductions and a timetable for a withdrawal from Iraq. Increasingly, the war in Iraq was seen as a distraction from the real war on terror which is taking place in Afghanistan.

Lernwortschatz   *task, postwar, to undertake, share, to restrict, consuming, position paper, prevention (of), to strain, tie (to/with), contribution (to), to restore (to), distorted, taboo, to deploy, troops, to patrol, combat, to involve, contemporary, sensitive (to), to prompt, to raise*

Discussion   *Germany's global role:* Inhaltlicher Perspektivwechsel – Kontrastierung mit der globalen Rolle der USA nach *9/11.* Methodisch: Interpretation von argumentativen Texten (Beispiele aus den ersten drei Topics ergänzen). Orientierungswissen zu der globalen Rolle der USA (S. 40), den vier Handlungsoptionen (S. 42), den Ereignissen vom 11. September 2001 (S. 40/41), den Unterschieden zwischen den folgenden kommentierenden Zeitungstexten: *editorial (= the (official) opinion of the editor/the newspaper) – comment (a journalist's opinion) – letter to the editor (a reader's opinion);* vgl. auch den Tipp zu *Editorial,* S. 45).

Pre-reading activity   ## 1 Before you read the editorial: Does Germany need an army?

Reaktivierung des Vorwissens und Erstellung eines Meinungsbildes nach der Methode: *think, pair, share,* d.h. Einzelarbeit (2 Minuten) – Partnerarbeit (4 Minuten) – Plenum (4 Minuten).

Alternative   Falls die Aufgabe als mündliche **Hausaufgabe** mit Notizen gestellt wird, folgt sofort Partnerarbeit. Falls sie als schriftliche **Hausaufgabe** erledigt wurde (je eine Hälfte des Kurses formuliert ein Pro- bzw. Contra-*Statement* zu *Why Germany needs/does not need an army.*), schließt sich die Partnerarbeit mit Pro-/Contra-Paaren an, danach folgen je zwei Präsenta-tionen vor der Klasse und anschließend eine Diskussion im Plenum (zwei S sichern wesentliche Argumente an der Tafel).

Lösungsvorschlag   ***Possible arguments for a German army and its tasks:*** *to ensure security at home, to defend/protect Germany against enemies/terrorists, to function as a stabilising force in German society, to participate actively in military/peace-building operations of NATO/the EU/the UN, etc.*
Possible arguments against a German army: *Germany's safety is not in danger any more, there are no external enemies any longer, the security of the country is guaranteed by NATO, Germany's history has shown that an army can easily become a tool of suppression, an army is never neutral and basically anti-democratic, etc.*

Discussion   ## 2 What global role does this New York Times editorial suggest ...

Die S notieren relevante Textstellen in zwei Spalten nach *suggestions* und *reasons.* Die Ergebnissicherung erfolgt über Folie oder Tafel.

Lösungsvorschlag   *Relevant phrases from the text:*

Lines	Quotes: Germany should ...
1–2	*... give up its "postwar pacifist mode" and "undertake a greater role in global security".*
3–4	*... "do its share of global peacekeeping and peacemaking."*

82

International peacekeeping Germany's army | **4**

Lines	Quotes: Germany should …
9–10	… become globally involved in "conflict prevention, peacekeeping and anti-terrorist actions".
16–19	… make "larger and more robust troop contributions".
26–28	… not only be involved in "reconstruction" but also in "combat".
33–34	… transform the Bundeswehr "into a global intervention force".

Reasons

- Germany is "the most populous European NATO country". (l. 18)
- Defending Germany's borders is no longer a real task in today's Europe. (ll. 4–6)
- Germany's allies, whose "military resources have been strained by multiple missions", need Germany's military support. (ll. 13–14)
- The political balance needs to be restored in view of Washington's overpowering role. (ll. 18–20)
- Historical post-war taboos have been falling steadily since 1992. (ll. 21–22)
- German militarism is a thing of the past. (l. 29)

Erweiterung Option zur Strukturierung des Textes: *Give headings to the five paragraphs (1.–5.)*

Lösungsvorschlag
1. A welcome announcement – greater global role for Germany
2. The expansion of Germany's global role is important/necessary
3. Germany's relationship to the United States
4. Historical taboos
5. From militarism to sensitivity to wrongdoing

Giving a speech | **3 Give a short speech in which you argue …**

Vorab Wiederholung der *Useful phrases* zu *Rhetorical devices* (S. 32).

Lösungsvorschlag Individuelle Beiträge.

Text production | **4 Suggest a BBC TV news item which this photo might accompany …**

Die S finden Beispiele entweder bei BBC oder CNN. L-Hinweis: *The photo needs to fit the news item, e.g. the German army acting in a Muslim country on a peacekeeping or peacemaking mission – a crisis situation in which the German army was involved – a politician has announced a policy change for the German army.*

Lösungsvorschlag *A suicide bomber has attacked a German army convoy in the city of Mosul in northern Afghanistan, wounding two soldiers. Afghan police securing the convoy opened fire on a crowd of demonstrators who showed their support for the attack by throwing stones and setting tents on fire. Six civilians were killed and several others wounded. The event happened against a background of increasing violence in parts of Afghanistan formerly considered to be relatively secure. In response to recent attacks, security measures have been tightened and the deployment of further troops is now seriously debated. Of late, the American President has increased pressure on Germany to take a more active role in Afghanistan in other regions of the country where they are more likely to be involved in open combat.*

Erweiterung Kontrastierung: *TV news item (short, factual, informative report on a topical event) vs. TV comment (subjective opinion on this event).* Mögliche **Hausaufgabe:** Schreiben und Vortragen eines Fernsehkommentars zu einer ausgewählten Nachricht. Der Austausch der Nachrichten erfolgt in Partnerarbeit.

83

4 International peacekeeping The European Union then and now

Comparison

5 Look again at the four options on page 42 ...

Wiederholung und Vergleich mit den USA.

Lösungsvorschlag

Option 1: For historical reasons, a leadership role is inacceptable for Germany.

Option 2: A focus on Germany's main interests is legitimate. However, this does not justify military intervention.

Option 3: Cooperation with our allies within NATO and the EU is essential. It is in Germany's interest to strengthen the UN's role; Germany should take on an active role, e.g. as a mediator in global trouble spots, and seek a permanent seat on the UN Security Council.

Option 4: Focusing exclusively on the protection of the German homeland is no realistic option for a country whose security is based on cooperation in NATO and the EU.

Political cartoon/ Map/Extract

| **The European Union then and now** | **pp. 46/47** |

HINTERGRUNDINFO

Historic milestones of the European Union

1951: The European Coal and Steel Community is established by the six founding members Belgium, Germany, France, Italy, Luxembourg and the Netherlands.

1957: The Treaty of Rome establishes a wider common market in the European Economic Community (EEC).

1973: First enlargement: The Community expands to nine member states (new: Denmark, Ireland, the United Kingdom).

1979: The first direct elections to the European Parliament (to be held every five years).

1981/1986: The first (Greece) and second (Spain, Portugal) Mediterranean enlargement.

1993: Completion of the single market.

1993: The Treaty of Maastricht establishes the European Union (EU), adding further areas of cooperation within integrated Community institutions.

1995: The EU expands to 15 members (new: Austria, Finland, Sweden).

2002: Euro notes and coins are introduced in twelve of the 15 member states, commonly referred to as the euro zone (not in Denmark, Sweden and the United Kingdom).

2004: Ten more countries join the Union: the former Soviet-bloc countries the Czech Republic, Hungary, Poland and Slovakia, the three Baltic states Estonia, Latvia, Lithuania, as well as Slovenia, Cyprus and Malta.

2007: Bulgaria and Romania join the EU.

2008: The euro zone consists of 15 countries. The twelve countries of the European Union that do not use the euro are: Denmark, Sweden, the United Kingdom, Bulgaria, the Czech Republic, Estonia, Hungary, Latvia, Lithuania, Poland, Romania and Slovakia. The next enlargement will be Slovakia in 2009.

"Europe in 12 lessons" is a brochure published by the European Commission in 2006. Its aim is to give an overview of the history, the present and future of the European Union. It was written by Pascal Fontaine, who is a professor at the Institute d'Études Politiques in Paris. The structure of the European Union, whose aim is to bring peace, prosperity and freedom for the 27 member states, is historically unique. There are three main bodies:

The European Parliament
- represents the people,
- shares legislative and budgetary power with the Council of the EU.

The Council of the EU or the Council of Ministers
- represents member states,
- the Council presidency is held by one member country for six months,
- main decision-taking body.

The European Commission
- represents common interest of the EU,
- main executive body,
- has the right to propose legislation/ensures that EU policies are properly implemented.

Lernwortschatz

to target, patriot, enlargement, to establish, single, prosperity, to overcome, balanced, challenge, to preserve, to uphold, respect, to represent, power, to propose, to implement, trafficking, to remain, proximity (to), development, to outline

Materialien → Online-Link: 601002-0022

International peacekeeping The European Union then and now | 4

Discussion *The global role of the European Union:* Erneuter inhaltlicher Perspektivwechsel – Kontrastierung mit den globalen Rollen der UN, NGOs, USA und Deutschland. Methodisch: Alle Aufgaben bereiten die *keynote speech to the European Parliament* (Aufgabe 7) vor, mit Rückgriff auf zuvor behandelte *global players*.

Describing a picture

1 What problem does the first cartoon target?

Warm-up und Aufhänger für Aufgabe 2. Evtl. kurze Beschreibung der Situation. Zur Bewertung/ Einschätzung des Problems Verweis auf die *Useful phrases* zu *Talking about problems*.

Lösungsvorschlag *Two characters on a bench in a park nearby an EU building. The young man is slouching on the bench – his body language (slouching position, eyes invisible behind long hair) indicates his lack of interest and enthusiasm.*
Message: *The younger generation has little political interest in the EU – indifference towards this institution – ignorance of how the EU works and what its aims are.*

Giving a statement

2 What does Europe mean to you?

Beschreibung des eigenen Verhältnisses zur EU. Wichtige Wörter: *I see myself more/rather as a … than …/neither as … nor …/both as … and …; relationship to/attitude to; patriotism/ patriotic/patriot; indifference/indifferent/(towards); interest in/enthusiasm about/ignorance of (the EU); a citizen of Germany/the EU; etc.*

Lösungsvorschlag Individuelle Antworten.

Analysis

3 Point out and explain the different attitudes …

Verweis auf *Useful phrases* zu *Talking about attitudes* (S. 47). Sicherung der Ergebnisse zu Aufgabe **a)** im Kursgespräch mit Tafelbild. Aufgabe **b)** erfolgt in arbeitsteiliger Partnerarbeit mit anschließender Präsentation im Plenum. Bewertungskritierien für die Dialoge: *acting in role – use of language – arguments – interaction/turn-taking.*

Lösungsvorschlag

a)

	The young generation	*The older generation*	*Widespread attitude in the population*
Attitude to the EU	*indifference, apathy, no interest*	*gratitude, support*	*benevolent acceptance: appreciation of free trade/open borders; but: often stereotypical views/limited knowledge*
Explanations	*no experience of WW II, peace and prosperity are taken for granted, the EU does not deal with young people's concerns and problems, etc.*	*historical perspective: the EU stands for peace and prosperity in post-war Europe, etc.*	*too many countries, limited travelling experience, little awareness of common values and aims, etc.*

b) Individuelle Dialoge.

Comprehension

4 What do you know about the EU?

Erste Anordnung mit Basiswissen/Logik/Karte in Gruppenarbeit. Formulieren von offenen Fragen: *What countries were the six founding members of the EU? Who is not a member yet?*

4 International peacekeeping Two ambassador's letters

Überprüfung der Antworten entweder als Hausaufgabe (Recherche) oder über die **Hintergrundinfos** zur EU (S. 84).

Lösungsvorschlag

1951:	1. European Coal and Steel Community (six founding members)
1957:	2. The Treaty of Rome – common market
1979:	3. The first direct elections
1993:	4. Completion of the single market; the Treaty of Maastricht – European Union
1995:	8. The EU expands to 15 members
2002:	5. Euro notes and coins
2004:	6. Ten more countries join the EU (25 members now)
2007:	7. Bulgaria and Romania join the EU

Discussion **5 Accepting the European Union as a reality, ...**

Vorstellen der individuellen Prioritätenlisten und Vergleich der Lösungen im Kursgespräch.

Lösungsvorschlag Individuelle Äußerungen mit Begründungen.

Research **6 The European Union is often criticized for its inefficiency.**

Die Vertiefung kann durch S-Referat erfolgen.

Lösungsvorschlag Siehe **Hintergrundinfos** zur EU, S. 84.

Discussion **7 To what extent is the European Union a global player?**

Präsentation/Lesen der Reden in Gruppenarbeit. Kriterienorientierte Auswahl der besten Rede für die Präsentation vor dem Kurs.

Lösungsvorschlag Individuelle Lösungen.

Erweiterung Aktualisierung der Mitgliedsstaaten mit Hilfe der Karte.

Letters to the editor

[8/9 ◎] Two ambassador's letters   p. 48

HINTERGRUNDINFO

Special relationship between the UK and the USA
The phrase "special relationship" is used to describe the largely positive political, diplomatic, cultural and historical relations between the United States and the United Kingdom. The phrase "special relationship" originated in a 1946 speech by Winston Churchill. The relationship between Tony Blair (British prime minister from 1997 to 2007) and George W. Bush (American president from 2001 to 2009) increased the importance of the United Kingdom for the United States, especially when, following the September 11 attacks, the UK proved to be the closest ally of the USA in the war on terrorism. However, Blair's unquestioning support for Bush and Britain's involvement in the war in Iraq damaged his reputation at home and in the rest of Europe. A June 2006 poll in "The Times" showed that the number of Britons supporting a special relationship with America had fallen to 58% and

that 65% believed Britain's future to lie more with Europe than America. A 2008 poll by "The Economist" has shown that Britons' views on religion, values, and national interest differ considerably from Americans' views. At the same time, 74% of Americans view Great Britain as their closest ally in the war in Iraq, with next-ranked Canada at 48%.

Robert H. Tuttle (born 1943) has held his post as ambassador of the United States in London since 2005. He graduated from Stanford University and received his master's degree from the University of Southern California. He was appointed Assistant to the President in 1982 and became Director of Presidential Personnel in 1985. Before starting his political career, he was co-managing partner of the Tuttle-Click Automotive Group, which is one of the larger automobile dealer organisations in the

International peacekeeping Two ambassador's letters **4**

United States. Tuttle is most widely known for his refusal to pay the London congestion charge (followed by a debate about whether the charge is a kind of taxation or just a fee for provided services).

***Wolfgang Ischinger** (born 1946) joined the German Foreign Service in 1975 after receiving his German law degree. Later, he earned his master's degree*

from Fletcher School of Law and Diplomacy. His diplomatic career started in the UN secretariat in New York; later he was sent to Washington D.C. and Paris. Ischinger served in various senior positions in the foreign ministry and is well-known for his participation in the negotiations regarding the Kosovo conflict. Since March 2006 he has been the ambassador for Germany in England.

Lernwortschatz *ambassador, relationship, to withstand, dilemma, united, liberty, rule of law, to value, to address, poverty, oppression, tie, to promote, benefit, advocate, recognised, to pull one's weight, leading, crisis, to appreciate, approach, to pool, agenda, equipped, opportunity*

Materialien → CD, Tracks 8/9

Discussion *The UK's relationship to the USA and Europe:* Inhaltlich ein erneuter Perspektivwechsel – die globale Rolle des *United Kingdom*, insbesondere die Beziehungen zu den USA und zu Europa. Methodisch: Strukturiertes Argumentieren und Kommentieren in Form von formalen Briefen. Einstieg über den Rückbezug auf die Statistiken (S. 44): *What do the statistics say about the UK's opinion of the US, the Americans and America's motives for its war on terrorism? Compare the figures with those of Germany.* Klären der besonderen Beziehung: *To what extent do the UK and the USA have a "special relationship"? Think of history and current conflicts.* Anschließend

[8/9 ◎] Präsentation von **Track 8/9** mit Hörauftrag: *Listen for the arguments in favour of a special US–UK relationship and a closer UK–EU relationship.*

Comprehension **1 *With the help of the two ambassadors' viewpoints …***

Verweis auf die *Fact file* zu *The UK and Europe*. Textverständnis der zwei Briefe und der *Fact file* durch *scanning* nach Pro-Argumenten. Mögliche Hausaufgabe: Sammeln der Argumente im Raster und Umsetzung in zwei kohärenten Absätzen.

Lösungsvorschlag

Arguments in favour of …

a) a special US–UK relationship:	b) a closer UK–EU relationship:
• *two centuries strong (ll. 1–2)* • *it has survived many historical crises and challenges (ll. 4–7)* • *shared values (l. 8)* • *reliable partners in addressing current problems (ll. 10–11)* • *close ties between the British and American people (ll. 13–14)* • *best friends (l. 16)*	• *helpful to promote European interests in the USA (ll. 3–6)* • *leading role of the UK in EU foreign and security policy (ll. 9–10)* • *global challenges demand combined resources and speaking with one EU voice (ll. 12–18)* • *hope of the UK being a strong and positive force in Europe (ll. 22–24)*

Analysis **2 *Collecting arguments***

Sukzessive Erarbeitung: Einzelarbeit – Partnerarbeit – Gruppenarbeit – Kursgespräch (ggf. arbeitsteiliges Vorgehen).

Lösungsvorschlag ***Possible arguments against a close US–UK relationship:***
It widens the gap to continental Europe/isolates Britain within Europe.
It isolates Britain in a world which perceives the UK as an uncritical US ally. etc.
Possible arguments against a close UK–EU relationship:
It limits national sovereignty.
It may lead to giving up the British pound.
It endangers the close UK–US relationship. etc.

87

4 | International peacekeeping   The world in 2031

Text production   ## 3 Letter to the editor

Wiederholung der Textsorte unter Rückgriff auch auf die *Useful phrases* zu *Writing a letter to the editor.*

Lösungsvorschlag   Individuelle Texte.

Erweiterung   **Alternative Textsorten zur Auswahl**

1. *(Personal) four-paragraph comment (introduction – pro-arguments – counter-arguments – conclusion)*
2. *Essay (provocative topic/thesis, e.g. "Why the UK should put its national interests first.")*
3. *Short talks (at a conference: various speakers/perspectives, e.g. Robert H. Tuttle, Wolfgang Ischinger, a Europhile or a Eurosceptic, etc.)*
4. *Podiumsdiskussion (Panel discussion: Britain's global role – alternatives and perspectives).*

Newspaper article   ## [10 ◉] The world in 2031   p. 49

HINTERGRUNDINFO

For 9/11: see **Hintergrundinfo**, *p. 70.*

For hot spot **Middle East:** see **Hintergrundinfo**, *p. 60.*

China and India: *The new popular term "Chindia" refers to China and India together in general, and their economies in particular. China and India are geographical neighbours and together have about one-third of the world's population. They are both among the fastest growing economies in the world and are the nations with the highest potential for growth in the next 50 years. They complement each other perfectly: while China is strong in manufacturing and infrastructure, India is strong in services and information technology; China is stronger in hardware while India is stronger in software. However, there are also political* *differences between China and India, with China being ruled by a single party and India being the world's most populous democracy.*

Paul Kennedy *(born 1945) is professor of British history at Yale University and since 2007 also professor of History and International Affairs at the London School of Economics. His most famous book is "The Rise and Fall of the Great Powers" (1987), which has been translated into 23 languages. In 2006 "The Parliament of Men: The United Nations and the Quest for World Government" was published and received positive reviews. His article in "The Independent" was a response to an article by the Harvard academic Niall Ferguson. In it Ferguson offers an optimistic description of what our world will look like 30 years after the 9/11 attacks.*

Lernwortschatz   *to attempt (to do sth), to reflect (on), aftermath, sabotage, administration, to recall, subsequent, to justify, to unfold, gloomy, assumption, to regard (as), unquestionably, overstretched, to grapple*

Materialien   → CD, Track 10/11

Discussion   Zusammenfassung der unterschiedlichen globalen Rollen und Perspektiven – Ausblick in die Zukunft (Prognose). Vorab Wiederholung des nötigen Orientierungswissens: *9/11*, die Entwicklung des Terrorismus in der Welt und die globale Rolle der USA, die Probleme Afrikas, die Visionen der EU und der UNO, die Aufgaben der NGOs.

Pre-reading activity   ## 1 Before you read

Reaktivierung von Vorwissen/Unterrichtsergebnissen zu *9/11.* Mögliche **Hausaufgabe** mit Bezug zur Gegenwart: *What has happened since then in the Middle East/Europe/Asia/North America? How has global terrorism developed?* Danach Präsentation des 1. Teils des Textes [10 ◉] entweder als Lesetext oder von der CD (**Track 10**) als *Listening comprehension: Does the text meet your expectations/predictions?*

Lösungsvorschlag   Siehe **Hintergrundinfos**, S. 70.

International peacekeeping The world in 2031 | 4

Alternative Statt Aufgabe 1 alternativer Einstieg über die Beschreibung der beiden Bilder und Bezug-setzung zum Titel *The world in 2031: Suggest captions (e.g. the urban metropolis of the future – space tourism)*. Die S stellen Vermutungen zum Inhalt des Textes an: *Make predictions about what the text might deal with.*

Analysis ## 2 From what perspective is this article written?

Aufdecken der Autorenperspektive. Möglich als *Pre-reading*-Aufgabe oder als nachträgliche Thematisierung.

Lösungsvorschlag *The author pretends to be writing in the year 2031 (l. 1). Against the background of the gloomy predictions for the world in 2001 and major political tendencies in global affairs at that time, he claims to know how the world actually changed in the following 30 years. This perspective gives the text a touch of science fiction.*

Text production ## 3 What events and tendencies does the author describe ...

[10◉] Auch möglich als Hörverstehen (**Track 10**) nur mit der CD.

Lösungsvorschlag *Three events (ll. 9–11)*
- *wars in Afghanistan, Iraq and Iran*
- *emergency military expeditions to defend Middle East oil fields*
- *a large number of terrorist attacks on the western world*

Six tendencies (ll. 18–25)
- *United States as the global leader*
- *Asia rising economically and militarily, esp. China and India*
- *Russia is recovering its place in world affairs*
- *Europe getting older and slower but still a nice place to live*
- *Africa faced with more disasters*
- *the Middle East unable to manage the 21st century*

Comprehension ## 4 [11◉] What do you think will happen between now and 2031?

Lernwortschatz *to disrupt, impact, setback, restraint, commitment (to), to endure, genocide, calamity, simultaneous, devastation, counterstrike, paralysed, moderate, to gain, promising, distant, belligerent*

[11◉] Die Vorhersagen der S zu Aufgabe **a)** an der Tafel oder auf Folie sichern. Danach erstes Vorspielen von **Track 11** (nur auf CD vorhanden) und Fragen zum Globalverstehen. Nach dem zweiten Vorspielen Vergleich der eigenen Vorhersagen mit den Textaussagen. Für ein detaillierteres Textverstehen ggf. anschließend Einsatz des *Tapescript* (steht als PDF auf der **CD-ROM** CD-ROM zur Verfügung).

Lösungsvorschlag a) Individuelle Lösungen (mit Blick auf die sechs Tendenzen und bezogen auf Staaten und Regionen).

b) *Most of the tendencies have continued, with the exception of the Middle East where violence erupted into civil wars and there were nuclear strikes between Iran and Israel.*

c) *The author's descriptions (in keywords)*
- *United States: still the global leader – now policies of cooperation.*
- *China and India: responsible global actors.*
- *Europe: self-doubts but "doing fine".*
- *Africa: more violence and disasters until the middle of the second decade, then slow progress in some parts of the continent.*
- *The Middle East: eruption of violence between 2009 and 2012 with collapsing regimes, worsening civil wars and nuclear strikes between Iran and Israel.*

4 International peacekeeping   The world in 2031

Evaluation

5 [♙♙♙] *Making a news programme: ...*

Materialien

→ Klausurvorschlag 4 • Revision file 4

Erarbeitung z. B. in 6 Gruppen, je 3 zu *utopian/dystopian scenarios*. Möglicher Zeitplan:
1. Stunde: Vorstellen der Aufgabe, Gruppenbildung, erste Absprachen/Ideen/Aufgaben für zu Hause; 2./3. Stunde: Arbeit in Gruppen/Proben/Aufnahmen; 4./5. Stunde: Präsentationen mit Auswertung. Mögliche Vorgaben/Entscheidungen/Absprachen:

- *Medium: radio programme or TV programme?*
- *Components: 4–6 news items (of global relevance) on events in different areas of the world; two comments; other components, e.g. eye-witness statements, expert reports (on location or in the studio), interviews, etc.*
- *Presentation: Live in the classroom or pre-recorded/videotaped? All group members take part in different roles, e.g. newsreader, expert, eye-witness, reporter on location, etc.*

Erweiterung

Zum Abschluss des *Topics* füllen die S *Revision file 4* (Themenheft, Seite 62) aus. Ein Lösungsvorschlag befindet sich hier im Lehrerbuch (Seite 120).

Sequenzplaner – Differenzierungshinweise GK/LK

Topic 1: Global challenges — p. 4–17

Titel	SB-Seite/ Unterrichts-stunden	Textsorte	Thema	Kernsequenz (GK +LK)/ Vertiefung (LK)
Global challenges	SB, S. 4/5 1 Stunde	Combination of visuals	Introduction to global challenges	Kernsequenz 1 (GK + LK)
Globalization blues	SB, S. 5 1 Stunde	American song	Protest song	Vertiefung 1 (LK)
The three eras of globalization	SB, S. 6/7 2 Stunden	American book excerpt (non-fiction)	History of globalisation	Kernsequenz 2 (GK + LK)
Spot on facts	SB, S. 8 1–2 Stunden	Fact file on globalisation	Definition of globalisation, basic global trends, hopes and fears	Vertiefung 2 (LK)
The corporation	SB, S. 9 1–2 Stunden	Canadian documentary film	Economic globalisation: corporations as "legal persons"	Kernsequenz 3 (GK + LK)
Sourcing global talent in software	SB, S. 10/11 1 Stunde	American news-paper interview	(Out)scourcing global talents	Vertiefung 3 (LK)
Cartooning outsourcing	SB, S. 11 1 Stunde	Cartoons	Cartooning outsourcing	
Moving goods around the globe	SB, S. 12/13 3 Stunden	British magazine article	The role of global transport	Kernsequenz 4 (GK + LK)
Frischer Wind für Frachter (Mediation)	SB, S. 14 1 Stunde	German magazine article	Reducing CO_2 emissions	Vertiefung 4 (LK)
My global mind	SB, S. 15 1 Stunde	American song	General global challenges	
Is American culture 'American'?	SB, S. 16/17 3 Stunden	American scholarly article	Cultural globalisation: America's role in the world's cultures	Kernsequenz 5 (GK + LK)

Topic 2: Think globally, eat locally? — pp. 18–23

Titel	SB-Seite/ Unterrichts-stunden	Textsorte	Thema	Kernsequenz (GK + LK)/ Vertiefung (LK)
Think globally, eat locally?	SB, S. 18 2 Stunden	Combination of visuals	Introduction to global food choices	Kernsequenz 1 (GK + LK)
Eating with food miles in mind	SB, S. 19 1–2 Stunden	Internet news story	Food miles	Vertiefung 1 (LK)
Organic movement split over air-freighted food	SB, S. 20/21 3 Stunden	British newspaper article/Mind-map	The organic vs. local debate	Kernsequenz 2 (GK + LK)
Organic food's carbon footprint	SB, S. 22 1–2 Stunden	Letters to the editor/Cartoon	The organic vs. local debate	Vertiefung 2 (LK)
We feed the world (Mediation)	SB, S. 23 2 Stunden	Austrian documentary film		

Topic 3: Saving the planet — pp. 24–33

Titel	SB-Seite/ Unterrichts-stunden	Textsorte	Thema	Kernsequenz (GK + LK)/ Vertiefung (LK)
Saving the planet	SB, S. 24 1–2 Stunden	Combination of visuals/Quotations	Introduction to saving the planet	Kernsequenz 1 (GK + LK)

SP Sequenzplaner

Titel	SB-Seite/ Unterrichts-stunden	Textsorte	Thema	Kernsequenz (GK + LK)/ Vertiefung (LK)
'Credit cards' to ration individuals' carbon	SB, S. 25 1–2 Stunden	British newspaper article	Limiting carbon emissions	Vertiefung 1 (LK)
Red alert! Climate change takes its toll on Scotland	SB, S. 26/27 3 Stunden	British newspaper article	Climate change in Scotland	Kernsequenz 2 (GK + LK)
Global warming profits	SB, S. 28 1 Stunde	Canadian newspaper article	Al Gore and the environment	
Eine unbequeme Wahrheit (Mediation)	SB, S. 29 1 Stunde	German magazine article/Cartoon	Al Gore and the environment	Vertiefung 2 (LK)
A friend of the earth	SB, S. 30/31 3–4 Stunden	Novel excerpt	A writer's view of the environment	Kernsequenz 3 (GK + LK)
Severn Suzuki speaks in Rio	SB, S. 32 1 Stunde	Speech	A speech on saving the earth	
Let's not worry about climate change!	SB, S. 33 1 Stunde	Advertisement	Aviation and climate change	Vertiefung 3 (LK)

Topic 4: International peacekeeping   pp. 34–49

Titel	SB-Seite/ Unterrichts-stunden	Textsorte	Thema	Kernsequenz (GK + LK)/ Vertiefung (LK)
International peacekeeping	SB, S. 34/35 2 Stunden	Combination of visuals	Introduction to peace-keeping and the UN	Kernsequenz 1 (GK + LK)
Address at the Royal Institute of International Affairs	SB, S. 36/37 2 Stunden	Political speech	The future of the UN	
An NGO at work	SB, S. 38 2 Stunden	Website	Non-governmental organisations	Vertiefung 1 (LK)
The world today – spotlight on Africa	SB, S. 39 2 Stunden	Political cartoon	Africa: problems, conflicts, attractions	
The USA – a global superpower	SB, S. 40 2 Stunden	Combination of visuals (photos/poster/cartoon)	Global superpower USA, 9/11 and terrorism	Kernsequenz 2 (GK + LK)
Courtesy of the red, white and blue	SB, S. 41 1–2 Stunden	American song	Mood and self-image of the US in 2002	
America's role in the world: four options	SB, S. 42 1 Stunde	Education programme	America's global policy options	
Spot on facts	SB, S. 43 1–2 Stunden	Fact file on USA	American history: the US and the world	
The opinion of the USA abroad	SB, S. 44 1 Stunde	Statistics	The global image of the US	Vertiefung 2 (LK)
Germany's army	SB, S. 45 1–2 Stunden	Editorial	Germany's global role	
The European Union then and now	SB, S. 46/47 2 Stunden	Cartoons/Map	The European Union: history, mission, global role	
Two ambassadors' letters	SB, S. 48 1 Stunde	Letters to the editor	US–UK relationship, the UK and Europe	
The world in 2031	SB, S. 49 1–2 Stunden	Newspaper article	Looking into the future	Kernsequenz 3 (GK + LK)

KV 1: Global values/Global challenges

p. 8, ex. 1

Global values

a) [👥] Tick (✔) the boxes in the grid and compare your results with a partner.
   1. Which three values are most important to you and why?
   2. Which values do you think are shared by most Germans?
   3. What/Who has shaped these values?

b) [👥] Try to agree with your partner on your top five global values.
   1. Which values are most important for a peaceful world?
   2. How can leaders/nations/individuals promote these core values?

Values	1. My top values (✔)	2. German values (✔)	3. Global values (rank 1–5)	How to promote global values
beauty				
change				_____
close friendship				_____
freedom				_____
good health				_____
independence				_____
intact nature				_____
status				_____
success				_____
tolerance				_____
wealth				_____
wisdom				_____
…				_____
…				_____

Global challenges

a) [👥] Discuss the following questions with your partner.
   1. Are any of these challenges individual or national threats rather than global challenges? Why?
   2. What other global challenges can you think of?
   3. Which of them may lead to armed conflicts?

> terrorism – unemployment – poverty – nuclear conflict – world hunger –
> AIDS – dictators as leaders – ecological disasters – climate change –
> supply of natural resources – exploitation – migration – racism – …

b) Explain the differences. What are the three most important issues …?

Global challenges	… for you?	… for most Germans?	… for the western world?	… for people in developing countries?	_____ _____ ?
1.					
2.					
3.					

© Ernst Klett Verlag GmbH, Stuttgart 2008 | www.klett.de
Von dieser Druckvorlage ist die Vervielfältigung für den eigenen Unterrichtsgebrauch gestattet. Die Kopiergebühren sind abgegolten. Alle Rechte vorbehalten.

Abi Workshop Englisch
Globalisation Lehrerheft
ISBN 978-3-12-601012-2

Kopiervorlagen

KV 2: Globalisation – definitions
p. 8, ex. 2

a) *Compare the information in the first two fact boxes on page 8 of your textbook with the definition of globalisation in the box below. Which do you prefer, and why?*

b) *The third box on page 8 ("Hopes and fears") describes different reactions to globalisation. Use key phrases from that box to extend the definition below. Work with enumeration and start like this:*

However, attitudes towards globalisation differ sharply. Some people hope for … Others fear …

> **Globalisation (Globalization)** refers to the growing worldwide economic, technological and cultural interaction between cultures and economies. This becomes visible e.g. in
> - the increasing global mobility of people, including tourists, immigrants, refugees, and business travellers,
> - the global flow of money and goods between international markets and production sites,
> - the global spread (and clash) of ideas and values,
> - the global distribution of information that appears on computer screens, in newspapers, on television, and on the radio.
>
> The process of globalisation since World World II has been made possible by
> - technological progress, especially in transport, communications and production methods,
> - a period of undisrupted peace and stability in the Western world, with a few mostly regional conflicts outside of it,
> - the growing influence of larger political and economic units (e.g. NATO, the EU), which reduces the role of borders and nation states, and creates new opportunities.
>
> In today's global world, time and space are no longer a barrier, the world is becoming a global village. This process is usually considered to be unstoppable and inevitable.
>
> - However, attitudes towards globalisation differ sharply. _____
>
> _____
> _____
> _____
> _____
> _____
> _____
> _____

c) *Write a "short and sweet" dictionary definition of "globalisation" for a new online dictionary. The publisher allows you between 90 and 110 words.*

_____
_____
_____
_____

KV 3: Global food (word power)

p. 19, ex. 4

a) *Top collocations: Use all the words to form ten word combinations.
All collocations can be found on pages 18 and 19 in your textbook.*

Adjective/Noun	+ Noun	Useful collocations
organic	level	
cholesterol	pollution	
eating	food	
soil	techniques	
greenhouse	habit	
intensive	lifestyles	
food	dioxide	
accelerating	miles	
farming	farming	
carbon	gases	

b) *Tricky words: Solve this pronunciation crossword puzzle.
"Read" the phonetic transcription cues, then spell the word.
You will find all the words on pages 18 and 19 in your textbook.*

Across
1 [ˌdaɪəˈbiːtiːz]
2 [ɪnˈgriːdiənts]
3 [kwɪzˈiːn]
4 [əˈvɜːʃn]
5 [ˈsæmən]
6 [əˈspærəgəs]

Down
7 [ˌbaɪəʊdɪˈgreɪdəbl]

c) *Words in context: Use an extra piece of paper and write a newspaper article using as many of the collocations and words above as possible. Underline and count the collocations/words you have used.*

KV | Kopiervorlagen

KV 4: The global food system

p. 21, ex. 6

[👥/👥👥] *A non-profit NGO campaigning against the global food system is looking for ideas for a leaflet which aims to appeal to young people. In pairs or groups, develop computer-designed leaflets. Based on criteria, make a competition to find the best suggestion.*

a) *Criteria: What is important for a good leaflet (see pp. 51–52 for ideas)?*

An effective leaflet _____

_____

_____

_____

b) *Facts and figures: Check the information box. Which facts/figures do you want to focus on?*

The implications of a global food system

Transporting food up to 2,000 km from field to table has 14 serious consequences:

A. Environmental implications

1. **The depletion of non-renewable resources,** especially fossil fuels, by the global trade in food and goods.
2. **Air pollution:** 1/12 of global CO_2 emissions come from food transportation.
3. **Soil erosion** as a result of monocropping, i.e. growing the same crop (e.g. maize, soybeans or wheat) year after year on the same land.
4. **Global pesticide** use increased 1300% from 1945 to 1980.
5. **Water pollution:** Soil erosion and pesticides affect water quality. This, in turn, affects fish stocks and other wildlife.
6. **The loss of hedgerows, woodlots and wetlands** by industrial agriculture and urbanisation.
7. **Reduced diversity:** Today, the world relies on 20 crops for 90% of its food (e.g. wheat, sugarcane, potatoes, soybeans, rice).
8. **Garbage:** Foods are packaged so that they can travel long distances. Landfills grow every year and result in soil and water pollution.

B. Human Health implications

1. **Pesticide poisoning:** Chemical pesticides are toxic substances that penetrate fruits and vegetables and cannot be washed off.
2. **Toxic ingredients:** We eat pesticides, herbicides, fertilisers, etc. equal to our entire body weight every ten years.
3. **Loss of food vitality:** Food loses vitality and nutrients between harvest and consumption.

C. Economic implications

1. **Cost:** Transportation, refrigeration and storage of food increase the costs.
2. **Loss of farmers' livelihoods:** Big agricultural businesses buy the most fertile land. Small farmers lose their livelihood.
3. **Monopolies** control around 70 per cent of world agricultural trade. This reduces consumer choice and competitiveness.

Ideas for the leaflet

_____

_____

_____

_____

_____

_____

_____

_____

_____

_____

_____

_____

_____

_____

_____

_____

_____

c) *Find pictures or drawings to go with the text and layout your leaflet on a computer.*

KV 5: Climate change made easy

p. 24, ex. 2

[👥] *Use this simplified graph to explain climate change. Work with a partner and use these words/phrases:*

| to lead to | to result in | to cause | to influence | to increase |

| the effect/consequence is that … | to have the effect that … |

ATMOSPHERE

Greenhouse effect: Greenhouse gases allow incoming solar radiation to pass through the Earth's atmosphere. They also stop most of the outgoing infrared surface radiation from escaping into outer space. This is a natural process and keeps the Earth's average surface temperature at about 15 degrees centigrade.

rising levels of greenhouse gases in the atmosphere

emissions of
- carbon dioxide
- methane
- nitrous oxide
(greenhouse gases)

heating effect

global warming

EARTH

- burning of fossil fuels (oil, coal, gas) and wood (rain forests – deforestation)
- increase in cattle breeding

CLIMATE CHANGE, e.g. changes in
- temperatures
- rainfalls
- the probability of extreme weather events

industrial countries and rising economic powers (China, India)
high economic activity – prosperity

developing countries
low economic activity – poverty

effects:
- melting ice caps/glaciers
- rising sea levels
- flooding
- forest fires
- heat waves
- heat waves/droughts
- storms/hurricanes
- food/water shortage
- diseases
- …

counter-measures
- carbon emission limits/cuts/trading
- development of alternative technologies
- renewable energy
- changes in lifestyles
- …

KV 6: Environmentally sinning

p. 31, ex. 2

Make a timetable of a usual day and list your "environmental sins" and how you could avoid them.

	My environmental sins	How I could avoid them
6:30	Central heating:	
7:00	In the bathroom:	
7:15	What (not) to wear:	
7:30	Breakfast (to produce one glass of Brazilian orange juice it is estimated that 22 glasses of water are used in the process):	
7:45	Going to school:	
8:00	At school:	
12:30	Lunch:	
1:00	Phone a friend:	
3:00	Going home:	
4:00	You've got mail … (240 kg of fossil fuels are burned to make just one desktop computer, not to mention all the chemicals that go into it):	
4:30	Homework:	
6:00	Dinner:	
7:00	TV, video/computer games:	

KV 7: War and peace (words in context)

p. 35, ex. 6

a) *Find the five perfect collocations (= common word connections) in each of the four sections. Write and read out in the role of a news presenter a news story using some of these collocations in the context of a current global crisis or conflict. Use an extra piece of paper.*

worst-case	management
troop	scenario
crisis	war
conflict	deployment
guerilla	resolution

flexible	strategy
public	response
comprehensive	process
peace-building	opinion
decision-making	measures

solution	of
example	to
negotiations	on
interest	between
attack	in

to declare	negotiations
to commit	war
to conduct	crimes
to apply	risks
to take	sanctions

b) *Different perspectives: Match the words/phrases from the left with their euphemisms (= milder, more positive words) on the right. Then write and read out different radio news versions of the same event. Report on a conflict first from the perspective of the country attacked, then from the viewpoint of the attacking nation.*

Word/Phrase
spy
war
killing of civilians
terrorist/guerilla
suicide bomber
attack from your own side
unprovoked attack
forced retreat
occupying force
overthrow of a government
to kill
invasion
prisoner of war
to invade

Euphemism
armed conflict
martyr
agent
friendly fire
collateral damage
regime change
freedom fighter
tactical regrouping
to take out
pre-emptive strike
peacekeepers
to liberate
intervention
detainee

c) *Grammar revision: If-clauses*

1. *Use if-clauses to discuss different policy options:*
   If the United Nations/the USA/Germany took a more active part in …,
   If … declared war on …,
   If … applied a different approach to …,

   > If I **had** a choice,
   > I **would choose** peace.

2. *Use if-clauses to point out the consequences of different policies in the past:*
   If the United Nations/USA/Germany/… had supported ….,
   If … had not become involved in …,
   If … had decided to …/had been prepared to …,

   > If my enemy **had suggested** peace, I **would have accepted** it.

3. *Have a conversation about a current political conflict in which you discuss future options and past decisions. Use as many if-clauses as possible.*

Abi Workshop Englisch
Globalisation Lehrerheft
ISBN 978-3-12-601012-2

KV | Kopiervorlagen

KV 8: 24 discussion strategies (Card game – part I)   p. 39, ex. 2

[👥] *This is a card game to apply the discussion and moderating skills from page 55 of your textbook. Read the rules carefully and play the game. After trying out the game, discuss how it can be improved.*

The five steps of the game

1. Make a list of everyday topics you are familiar with, e.g. school, family, friends, books, computers, leisure activities, learning English, feature films, etc. Add more advanced topics from your lessons, e.g. globalisation, genetic engineering, the American Dream, etc.

2. Form groups of 5 (6) students. In each group, choose a chairperson (chair) and one topic from your list.

3. The chairperson cuts out the 24 strategy cards (KV 8a, p. 101) and puts them face down in the middle of the table. Each group member except the chair takes 6 (4–5) cards and places them on the table in front of himself/herself.

4. The person with the "beginning" card starts the discussion on the chosen topic with a short provocative statement. Then he/she gives this card to the chair.

5. The other group members try to get involved in the discussion by playing one of their strategy cards. To do this, they raise their hands and are then called up by the chair. Before they start to speak, they hand over the respective card for the chair to examine the strategy. The aim of the game is to get rid of one's cards as fast as possible. The game is over when all but one player have played their cards.

Additional rules

- A contribution to the discussion should include one of the phrases/sentences from the strategy card and be at least three sentences long.

- The chair decides whose turn it is to speak. If more than one player indicates his/her willingness to speak, the player with more cards has priority.

- The chair also checks if a player is taking part in the discussion according to his/her chosen strategy. If not (or if the statement is not long enough), the card is handed back to the player.

- The chair's authority is not to be questioned during the game. The chair may give additional cards to players who do not follow the rules.

- The "loser" (= the last player with cards) has the right to suggest a new topic and start a new game.

- The "winner" (= the first player without cards) is the new chair.

KV 8a: 24 discussion strategies (Card game – part II)   p. 39, ex. 2

[👥] *Read the rules on page 100 (KV 8) carefully and play the game. After trying out the game, discuss how it can be improved.*

Giving an opinion	Agreeing	Making suggestions
In my opinion/view … To my mind … I am of the opinion that … I am sure/convinced that …	Absolutely./Precisely./Exactly. I totally agree. I can go along with that. I think you are right to a point.	What about (+ gerund)? If I were you, I would … I would suggest/recommend that … I call for/demand …
Asking for an opinion	**Disagreeing**	**Supporting someone**
How do you feel about this? What is your view/position on …? I would be very interested to hear X's opinion on this.	I am sorry but I don't agree at all. I think you are wrong here. It isn't as simple as that. I believe X was mistaken when … I am afraid things are not as simple as X would have us believe.	That's a good idea. I fully support X's view. I wholeheartedly support X's statement. That sounds very convincing.
Beginning	**Ordering**	**Adding**
I would like to start with … Let me begin with … To start with, …	There are three points I would like to make. First of all, … Secondly, … Finally, …	I'd like to add that … What is also important to know is that … Another reason is that …
Emphasising	**Balancing**	**Drawing conclusions**
I would like to stress/underline/emphasise that … Let me repeat what I said earlier. What I strongly believe is that …	On the one hand …, but on the other (hand) … Although …, we mustn't forget that … That is certainly true, but at the same time it is obvious that …	That's why … /For this reason … As a result, … The logical consequence is that … This leads to … This implies that …
Interrupting politely	**Defending your point**	**Picking up someone's statement**
May I interrupt you for a second? Excuse me, could you explain that again? Sorry, can I just make a point?	That's not what I was trying to say. My point is that … I see your point but I still feel that … That's not quite what I mean. What I am saying is that …	I would like to come back to/comment on what X said about … If I may just remind you of what X said … As we have just heard from …
Dealing with interruptions	**Correcting misunderstandings**	**Introducing a new point**
I haven't finished yet if you don't mind. If I might just finish … I haven't got to my point yet.	I am afraid there has been some misunderstanding. What I actually said was … That's not quite what I meant by … Don't get me wrong. What I meant was …	I would like to raise another point. What we haven't discussed yet is the question whether/if … We should also discuss what this means for …
Checking understanding	**Giving evidence**	**Giving in (to some extent)**
Do you really mean to say that …? So, if I understand you correctly, … What exactly do you mean by that?	Statistics/Surveys show … Most scientists now agree that … There is strong evidence that … I know this from first-hand experience. I would like to draw your attention to the fact that …	Even if that is so, … That's probably true, but … Possibly, but …
Arguing against something	**Giving an example**	**Playing for time**
I strongly criticise … I completely disagree with you on … I would question that argument.	For instance, look at … Take …, for example. Let me give you an example of what I mean by … To illustrate this point, …	To be quite honest, … What I'm trying to say is that … So you mean that … I'm glad you asked me that question.

Lösungen zu den Kopiervorlagen

Kopiervorlage 3

a) *organic food, cholesterol level, eating habit, soil pollution, greenhouse gases, intensive farming, food miles, accelerating lifestyles, farming techniques, carbon dioxide*

b) **Across:** *1. diabetes, 2. ingredients, 3. cuisine, 4. aversion, 5. salmon, 6. asparagus;*
Down: *7. biodegradable*

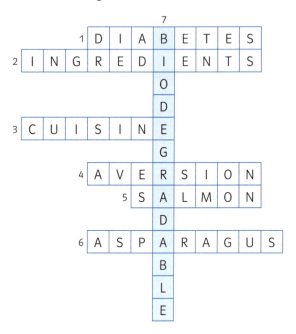

Kopiervorlage 7

a) 1. *worst-case scenario, troop deployment, crisis resolution, conflict management, guerilla war;*
2. *flexible response, public opinion, comprehensive strategy, peace-building measures, decision-making process;*
3. *solution to, example of, negotiations between, interest in, attack on;*
4. *to declare war, to commit crimes, to conduct negotiations, to apply sanctions, to take risks*

b) *spy – agent, war – armed conflict, killing of civilians – collateral damage, terrorist/guerilla – freedom fighter, suicide bomber – martyr, attack from your own side – friendly fire, unprovoked attack – pre-emptive strike, forced retreat – tactical regrouping, occupying force – peacekeepers, overthrow of a government – regime change, to kill – to take out, invasion – intervention, prisoner of war – detainee, to invade – to liberate*

Klausurvorschläge

Klausurvorschlag Topic 1: Tony Blair's *Lord Mayor's Banquet Speech*

During a traditional dinner at the Guildhall in London on November 14, 2005, British Prime Minister Tony Blair made a major world affairs speech.

Thirty years ago a political leader who said that the way to advance the national interest was through the spread, worldwide, of the values of democracy, justice and liberty, would have been called an idealist.
5   Today such a person is a realist. We describe the modern world as interdependent. We acknowledge the force of globalisation. But we fail to follow through the logic of these realities in global politics.
   Nations are deeply connected at every level. Of
10 course, economically, but also now through communication, travel and technology.
   Yesterday, by chance, I watched part of the MTV Music Awards. Well, it was certainly the most relaxed part of the week I just had. I recommend it to any
15 person who wants to understand modern politics. Why? There was no politics discussed. But the fusion of sounds, rhythms and musical influences from vastly different cultures was an allegory for today's world and the context in which politics exists. This is a world
20 integrating at a fast rate, with enormous economic, cultural and political consequences.
   And it all happens as a result of what people themselves are doing. Occasionally we debate globalisation as if it were something imposed by
25 governments or business on unwilling people. Wrong. It is the individual decisions of millions of people that is creating and driving globalisation. [...]
   Out of this great pumping up of global integration comes the need for stronger and more effective global,
30 multilateral action. There is a real danger that the institutions of global politics lag seriously behind the challenges they are called upon to resolve. These challenges are pressing. The most obvious is global terrorism.
35   Barely a week goes by without another country being added to the grieving list of victims. Jordan, Egypt, Indonesia, India and of course here in London. Recently, in Australia, it appears an attack was foiled. We have disrupted two groups planning attacks here in
40 the UK since 7 July alone. What is obvious now to all is that this is a global movement and requires global action in response, of which the successful completion of a democratic process in Afghanistan and Iraq is a major component. So is the push for peace between Israel and Palestine.
   In all of these conflicts, the only successful solution is based on democratic consent; and success would have a tremendous persuasive effect far beyond the frontiers of the countries concerned.
   Similarly, with the challenge of climate change, the world has to act together. After Gleneagles we began the G8 + 5 talks with the first meeting in London on November 1.
   The commitment period under the Kyoto protocol ends in 2012. We urgently need a framework, with the necessary targets, sensitively and intelligently applied over the right timeframe, that takes us beyond 2012.
   It can only happen if the US, China and India join with Europe, Japan and others to create such a framework. Failure will mean not only increasing the damage to the environment but in a world of greater competition for carbon fuel, real pressure on energy supply and energy prices. Yet such an agreement cannot materialize without the major nations of the world agreeing an approach that is fair and balanced. [...]
   In a modern world there is no security or prosperity at home unless we deal with the global challenges of conflict, terrorism, climate change and poverty. Self interest and mutual interest are inextricably linked. National interests can best be advanced through collective action.
   Calculate not just the human misery of the poor themselves. Calculate our loss: the aid, the lost opportunity to trade, the short-term consequences of the multiple conflicts; the long-term consequences on the attitude to the wealthy world of injustice and abject deprivation amongst the poor. We will reap what we sow; live with what we do not act to change.
Here, in the City of London, which makes its living above all by being the meeting point of many nations, and which through trade creates much of the wealth on which this British nation depends, is a good place for this call to action. So let us act.

(684 words)

KL Klausurvorschläge

Annotations

line 18: **allegory** – *here*: typical example
line 51: **Gleneagles** – a hotel in Scotland; *here*: the G-8 Summit in July, 2005, where the heads of government of Canada, France, Germany, Italy, Japan, Russia, the United Kingdom and the United States met to discuss international problems
line 52: **G8 + 5 talks** – the meeting of the eight politicians with the political leaders of Brazil, China, India, Mexico and South Africa
line 54: **commitment period** – a period of time for which plans and promises have been made
line 54: **the Kyoto protocol** – an international agreement from February 16, 2005, to reduce greenhouse gas emission worldwide

Tasks

1 Comprehension

Outline Tony Blair's view of globalisation, the global challenges of our time and necessary political answers.

2 Mediation

You have watched Tony Blair's speech on globalisation on television. A friend of yours asks you what Blair was talking about. Summarise (in German) what he said about globalisation, global challenges and political answers.

3 Analysis

Explain how the Prime Minister uses argumentative structure, language and rhetorical devices to convince the audience of his view on globalisation.

4 Evaluation

a) Evaluation: comment
   In lines 66–71 Tony Blair states:

   "In a modern world there is no security or prosperity at home unless we deal with the global challenges of conflict, terrorism, climate change and poverty. Self interest and mutual interest are inextricably linked. National interests can best be advanced through collective action."

   Comment on this statement and its implications for the richest countries and for yourself.

b) Composition/Text production
   After Tony Blair's speech, a political representative of India who is a guest of honour at the dinner is invited by the host, the Lord Mayor of London, to give a speech in response to the Prime Minister's speech.

   Write the speech.

5 Translation

Translate lines 35–45 of the speech into German (96 words). ("Barely a week … and Palestine.")

Klausurvorschlag Topic 2: Going the Distance: Food Miles and Global Warming

by Deborah Zabarenko

WASHINGTON – The U.S. local food movement – which used to be elite, expensive and mostly coastal – has gone mainstream, with a boost from environmentalists who reckon that eating what grows nearby cuts down on global warming.

But do food miles – the distance edibles travel from farm to plate – give an accurate gauge of environmental impact, especially where greenhouse gas emissions are concerned? "Food-miles are a great metaphor for looking at the localness of food, the contrast between local and global food, a way people can get an idea of where their food is coming from," said Rich Pirog, associate director of the Leopold Center for Sustainable Agriculture at Iowa State University.

"They are not a reliable indicator of environmental impact," Pirog said in a telephone interview. "What one would want to do is look at your carbon footprint across a whole food supply chain." The problem with food-miles is that they don't take into account the mode of transport, methods of production or the way things are packaged, and all of these have their own distinct impact on emissions of carbon dioxide, a climate-warming gas.

Take the case of the well-traveled Idaho potato and its closer-to-home cousin from Maine. For a consumer on the US East Coast, the Maine potato seems the winner in the local food derby. But Maine potatoes get to market by long-haul truck while Idahos go by train, a more energy-efficient mode of transportation, so they have a smaller carbon footprint even with a larger number of food-miles.

The example is easily transposed to Europe, Pirog said, noting the relative environmental impacts for a Stockholm consumer in tomatoes grown in a Swedish greenhouse compared with field-ripened tomatoes imported by ship from Spain. The Spanish tomatoes are more Earth-friendly. […]

The United States came late to the local food movement, except for high-end eateries that featured their offerings' provenance as a selling point in the 1970s. Until then, imported food was considered a status symbol, no matter what condition it was in when it finally arrived at the table. Before that, most Americans unthinkingly ate local food out of simple necessity. If your great-grandmother wanted a tomato in winter, she probably opened a home-canned jar rather than picking an Israeli-raised specimen at the supermarket.

Another difficulty with the food-miles measurement is that the most accurate versions of this calculation deal only with produce, not with prepared foods that contain many ingredients from many sources. […]

The calculus is not always environmental; most locavores say taste comes first, while some maintain locally produced products are safer or more nutritious. Others, like restaurateur Barry Eastman, say local provisions make economic sense for the businesses that use them and the farmers that raise them.

As the owner of Rudy's Tacos in Waterloo, Iowa, Eastman has been seeking out local suppliers for a decade, with 70 percent of his food produced in Iowa. This is not as obvious as it may seem: while Iowa is dense with farm fields, most are planted with commodity crops like soybeans and feed corn – a circumstance that makes parts of the state food deserts. Corn, corn everywhere, but not an ear to eat, if you're a human.

"You'd be surprised at how many people want to know where their food is coming from," Eastman said by telephone. "It's not just the granola bar folks, everybody's starting to get into it."

In his case, the primary driver was flavor, and he found that local chickens made for a better-tasting taco than those trucked in from Alabama in the same load with paper towels and other restaurant staples. The Iowa poultry cost more per bird but less overall because they were meatier, Eastman said.

Tim Schlitzer, executive director of the Food Routes Network, which promotes a national "Buy Fresh, Buy Local" consumer campaign, noted long-term reasons to encourage the locavore movement. As commodity farming increases in the United States, some regions can lose the ability to feed themselves, Schlitzer said in a telephone interview from Arnot, Pennsylvania. "Right now, there's a national and international food system," Schlitzer said. "Ten years, 20 years from now, will that still be the case?"

(704 words)

KL Klausurvorschläge

Annotations

line 6:	**edibles** – food that is safe or good enough to eat
line 7:	**gauge** – measurement, assessment
line 28:	**long-haul** – traveling a long distance
line 39:	**high-end eatery *(AE)*** – a restaurant that is more expensive than other restaurants
line 40:	**provenance *(fml)*** – origin
line 53:	**calculus** – type of mathematics used for calculating such things as the slopes of curves
line 54:	**locavore** – a person who will only cook and eat food grown locally
line 57:	**provisions** – food and other necessary supplies
line 64:	**commodity crops** – *Nutzpflanzen*
line 64:	**feed corn** – *Futtermais*
line 66:	**ear (corn)** – part of the top of a plant that contains the grain
line 70:	**granola *(AE)*** – muesli
line 72:	**driver** – *here:* sth that makes important things happen, e.g. in an organisation or economy
line 75:	**staples** – products, esp. foods that are the most basic and important
line 76:	**poultry** – birds such as chickens that are used for meat or eggs

Tasks

1 Contents/Comprehension

a) Summarise the text in not more than 200 words.

b) Give an account of the aspects that are important for the local food movement.

2 Form/Analysis

a) What means in language and style does the author use and what is their effect?

b) What is the attitude of the author and how does she show it?

3 Discussion/Comment

a) Discuss what you personally find more relevant, food miles or the carbon footprint of your food. Point out what impact your food choice can have on the environment.

b) "You'd be surprised at how many people want to know where their food is coming from."
(Barry Eastman)

Write an e-mail to Barry Eastman pointing out how food-conscious people in Germany are according to your opinion in comparison with what you read about Americans. Describe your attitude as well.

c) The local food mentioned in this article might not be organic. However, the organic food from your "Bioladen" might be air-freighted. Comment on this dilemma taking into consideration as many aspects as you can and point out your own opinion.

Klausurvorschlag Topic 3: Queen opens new $8.6 B airport terminal

LONDON, ENGLAND (CNN) – Queen Elizabeth helped launch Heathrow's $8.6 billion new Terminal 5 on Friday as part of the British airport's rejuvenation plan to maintain its status as one of the world's most important
5 transport hubs. The British monarch, who also opened Heathrow's first passenger terminal in 1955, was present under strict security a day after a man carrying a backpack was arrested for running onto a runway at the airport. [...]
10 Its opening has come after 15 years of planning and construction by its owners BAA – and protests by local residents and environmental groups. It is part of a strategy which could lead to passenger numbers almost doubling to 122 million a year, with a sixth terminal and
15 a third runway in the pipeline despite some vociferous opposition.

Spanish-owned BAA, which also runs Gatwick and Stansted in Britain, also plans to eventually demolish Terminals 1 and 2 and replace them in a project called
20 Heathrow East. Residents were once told by BAA that there would be no fifth terminal, but the company is planning to forge further ahead despite the concerns of environmental groups.

"Terminal 5 stands as a monument to the binge-
25 flying culture this Government has done so much to encourage," Greenpeace transport campaigner Anita Goldsmith told the UK Press Association. "It's part of an obsession with expansion which can only mean more flights, more emissions and more climate change."

Richard Dyer of Friends of the Earth added: "If the 30 Government is serious about tackling climate change, the opening of Terminal 5 must mark the end of airport expansion in Britain. Further expansion of Heathrow would be environmentally irresponsible and isn't necessary for the economy of London."

However, business groups welcomed the expansion 35 at Heathrow.

"Thriving, growing airports are vital to help maintain Britain's economic competitiveness," Neil Pakey, chairman of the Airport Operators' Association, told PA.

"Domestic air links to Heathrow are particularly 40 valuable for the regional economies, and this new terminal will undoubtedly provide them with a much-needed boost. The passage of the current Planning Bill must ensure that this is the last airport which has to endure such an absurdly protracted planning process." 45

Visit London chief executive James Bidwell said: "T5 will provide visitors to London and the UK with a spectacular first impression and alleviate the pressure experienced at Heathrow, the world's busiest airport. "The terminal's smoother check-in process and state-of- 50 the-art baggage management system will certainly better the tourist experience and should help improve the airport's international reputation."

(422 words)

The following table contains *United Kingdom Civil Aviation Authority* data from 2007 on the busiest UK airports including information on passenger traffic as well as aircraft movements and cargo volume handled at each airport.

2007 – 10 largest airports

Rank	Airport	IATA Code	International Passengers	Domestic Passengers	Transit Passengers	Total Passengers	Aircraft Movements	Freight (Metric Tonnes)
1	London Heathrow	LHR	62,098,911	5,753,476	213,641	68,066,028	481,476	1,310,987
2	London Gatwick	LGW	31,142,002	4,023,402	50,709	35,216,113	266,550	171,078
3	London Stansted	STN	21,204,946	2,554,304	20,447	23,779,697	208,462	203,747
4	Manchester	MAN	18,662,468	3,229,255	220,902	22,112,625	222,703	165,366
5	London Luton	LTN	8,427,894	1,491,467	7,960	9,927,321	120,238	38,095
6	Birmingham	BHX	7,592,240	1,541,815	92,285	9,226,340	114,679	13,585
7	Edinburgh	EDI	3,417,891	5,619,309	10,358	9,047,558	128,172	19,292
8	Glasgow	GLA	4,131,512	4,594,575	69,640	8,795,727	108,305	4,276
9	Bristol	BRS	4,608,290	1,275,566	42,918	5,926,774	76,428	20,000
10	Newcastle	NCL	3,948,594	1,675,013	27,109	5,650,716	79,200	785,000

Source: *United Kingdom Civil Aviation Authority*

KL Klausurvorschläge

Annotations

line 3: **rejuvenation** – making sth good and effective again
line 5: **hub** – a central airport from which you can make international and long-distance flights
line 15: **in the pipeline** – planned in order to happen soon
line 15: **vociferous** *(fml)* – expressing one's opinion loudly and with force
line 22: **to forge** – to keep moving forward
line 24: **binge** – doing too much of sth you enjoy; *here:* of flying
line 37: **thriving** – very successful
line 43: **boost** – improvement
line 45: **protracted** *(fml)* – lengthy
line 48: **to alleviate** *(fml)* – to relieve

Tasks

1 Contents/Comprehension

a) Summarise the text in not more than 150 words.

b) What are the main arguments for and against the new terminal?

2 Form/Analysis

a) How does the author try to be objective when reporting about the new terminal? To what extent does he succeed?

b) Choose some pieces of data from the chart and compare them. To what extent do they support the statements from the text?

c) What means in language and style does the author use to make the text interesting? Quote from the text to prove your findings.

3 Discussion/Comment

a) "Terminal 5 stands as a monument to the binge-flying culture this Government has done so much to encourage." (ll. 24–26)

Referring to this text and to what you know about low-cost airlines discuss the pros and cons of "binge-flying". Point out your own opinion about it.

b) Write an e-mail to James Bidwell, the chief executive of Visit London, and point out to what extent you think T5 will have an impact on tourism. Base your arguments on what you know about the topic and this text.

c) Imagine Richard Dyer of *Friends of the Earth* has asked you to support him with information and data about aviation in the UK. He also wants your opinion.

Write a report using the text and table as well as your knowledge of the topic.

Klausurvorschlag Topic 4: Ban Ki-moon: Address to the International Conference on Terrorism: Dimensions, Threats and Counter-Measures

In Tunis on 15 November, 2007, UN Secretary Ban Ki-moon made a keynote speech on terrorism to open an international conference.

Let me thank the President, Government and people of the Republic of Tunisia for graciously hosting this conference. Equally, I thank the Organization of the Islamic Conference (OIC), whose Islamic Educational,
5 Scientific and Cultural Organization (ISESCO) has been our steadfast partner in organizing it.

By collaborating in this way, we give life to the United Nations Global Counter-Terrorism Strategy, unanimously adopted by the UN General Assembly in
10 September 2006. The Strategy calls on us to make full use of the role which regional and other organizations can play in the global endeavour to counter terrorism. By cooperating here, we honour that call.

Beyond this hall, we are partners every day in the
15 struggle against terrorism, and in the work to implement the Global Counter-Terrorism Strategy. Organizations such as the OIC and ISESCO have indispensable expertise in the cultural and other contextual dimensions of that mission.

20 The adoption of the Strategy was a milestone. It was the first time that all 192 UN Member States came together to formulate a comprehensive, collective, and intergovernmentally approved plan to counter terrorism. It was the first time they agreed that
25 conditions exist that can be conducive to the spread of terrorism, and that, to gain ground, they must address these conditions. It was the first time they agreed that all Governments and organizations must convey the same critical message: terrorism is never justifiable,
30 whether on political, philosophical, ideological, racial, ethnic, religious or any other grounds.

This conference is an important opportunity to consolidate that achievement. It provides a venue for representatives from Europe, the Middle East, Asia,
35 North America, and elsewhere to engage with one another, and with the international community as a whole, on ways to advance the implementation of the Global Counter-Terrorism Strategy.

Conditions conducive to the spread of terrorism exist
40 on many fronts. They include:
- prolonged unresolved conflicts;
- dehumanization of victims;
- lack of rule of law and violations of human rights;
- ethnic, national and religious discrimination;
45 - political exclusion;
- social and economic marginalization; and
- lack of good governance.

Such conditions may be local in origin, but they have consequences for all States.

50 Terrorists may exploit vulnerabilities and grievances to breed extremism at the local level, but they can quickly connect with others at the international level. Similarly, the struggle against terrorism requires us to share experiences and best practices at the global level. And
55 by jointly addressing conditions conducive to the spread of terrorism, we can complement international cooperation on security and law enforcement. Let me be clear: when we stand up for human rights, combat poverty and marginalization, when we seek to resolve
60 conflicts, support good governance and the rule of law, we do so because these activities have intrinsic value and should be pursued in their own right.

But as we do, we also work to counter terrorism, by addressing the very conditions that can be conducive to
65 it.

The United Nations stands ready to assist on many fronts, including setting standards and sharing lessons learnt among all nations. Member States now have a more coherent, more directed, and more user-friendly
70 partner in the United Nations system.

The United Nations Counter-Terrorism Implementation Task Force illustrates how the United Nations family can work as one. We are working with Member States in mapping and analysing national and
75 international initiatives for addressing radicalization and recruitment; in advancing the protection of human rights; in helping to protect vulnerable targets; and in addressing the needs of victims of terrorism.

The United Nations is also working with Member
80 States to build an Alliance of Civilizations, an initiative in which many of you here have been so constructively engaged. This is a crucial component in addressing the religious, cultural and social issues often exploited by extremists – a particular focus of this conference.

85 The UN's 192 Member States made history just over one year ago when they adopted the Strategy as a visionary yet practical guide for international activities to counter terrorism. Yet our work together is just beginning. Now we must implement the Strategy in all
90 its dimensions. By next September, when the General Assembly meets to review implementation of the strategy, we must all have concrete progress to show – Member States, the United Nations system, and our key partners in regional and other organizations.

95 The more we bring leaders together in an ongoing exchange – to share best practices, to thrash out differences, to raise awareness – the better we can build understanding, respect and dialogue among societies, cultures, religions and nations. And the more
100 effectively and comprehensively we can work to implement our Global Counter-Terrorism Strategy. I look to this Conference to set us decisively on that path.

(783 words)

KL Klausurvorschläge

Annotations

line 3–4: Organization of the Islamic Conference (OIC) – an international organization with 57 Islamic member states from all over the world and a permanent delegation to the United Nations; its Islamic Educational, Scientific and Cultural Organization (ISESCO) aims to promote cooperation amongst member states in various fields within the framework of Islamic values and ideals, and to uphold international peace and security

Tasks

1 Comprehension

Describe the historical context of the speech and point out the topics and aims of the conference as well as the role of the United Nations.

2 Mediation

A German reporter present at the opening of the conference informs the editor of his newspaper about the topics and aims of the conference as detailed in Ban Ki-moon's introductory keynote speech. Summarise his speech in German.

3 Analysis

Explain the way in which Ban Ki-moon sets the tone for the conference. In doing so, examine the structure, content and language of the speech.

4 Evaluation

a) Evaluation: comment
With reference to the Ban Ki-moon speech from November 2007 and the current political situation in the world, discuss some of the conditions conducive to terrorism (l. 41–47) and the chances of international cooperation in combating terrorism.

b) Composition/Text production
Write an article for a British/American quality newspaper reporting on the opening of the conference in Tunisia the day before and commenting on its relevance in the struggle against terrorism.

5 Translation

Translate lines 50–62 of the speech (108 words) into German. ("Terrorists may exploit vulnerabilities … pursued in their own right.")

Erwartungshorizont zu den Klausurvorschlägen

Topic 1: Textinformation

Autor: Tony Blair
Titel: Lord Mayor's Banquet Speech, 14 November 2005
Quelle: www.number-10.gov.uk/output/Page8524.asp (geprüft: 16.06.2009)
Textformat/Textlänge: Sachtext (politische Rede), 681 Wörter

Erwartungshorizont

1 Comprehension

- Aspects of globalisation as a process which (according to Blair): connects nations globally and makes them interdependent at every level/happens fast and with enormous effects/individuals participate and share.
- Blair points out global challenges e.g. global conflicts and terrorism, climate change, poverty, competition for carbon fuel.
- As a political answer to these global challenges, Blair demands a framework which is strong and effective/is fair and balanced/is globally agreed on/has a long-term timeframe with clear targets.
- Blair regards this framework as necessary because
  - it serves the national interests (security and prosperity),
  - if not agreed on – this would have negative consequences (e.g. pressure on energy supply and prices),and be a sign of moral indifference.

2 Mediation

Blair sieht die Globalisierung als Prozess, der Nationen global verbindet und Interdependenzen in vielen Bereichen schafft/der schnell und unaufhaltsam abläuft und weitreichende Auswirkungen hat/an dem jeder Einzelne beteiligt ist. Blair hat Beispiele für globale Herausforderungen gegeben, z.B. Terrorismus und Konflikte mit überregionaler Bedeutung, Klimawandel, Armut, die Nachfrage nach Brennstoffen. Blair hat einen Rahmenplan als Antwort auf diese globalen Herausforderungen gefordert, der umfassend und effektiv ist, fair und ausgewogen im Ausgleich der Interessen, im Konsens aller Beteiligten vereinbart wird sowie langfristig angelegt ist mit eindeutig formulierten Zielen. Blair schätzt diesen Rahmenplan als unbedingt notwendig und dringlich ein, da er dem nationalen Interesse entspricht (Wahrung von Sicherheit und Wohlstand)/ein Scheitern einer Einigung tiefgreifende negative Auswirkungen hätte, beispielsweise auf die Energieversorgung und den Energiepreis, und zudem ein Zeichen moralischer Gleichgültigkeit wäre.

3 Analysis

- Clear text structure – sections e.g. introduction to the topic (historical development) – description of globalisation and example – appeal/thesis – global challenges (examples and answers) – self interest and national interest in the topic – call to action.
- Main argumentative device: antithesis/contrast (to point out developments or alternatives) e.g. "thirty years ago/today"/"… something imposed by … Wrong. It is …"/"Globalisation isn't something done to us. It is something we are … doing to and for ourselves."
- Clear and graphical language which is instantly understandable, e.g. figurative phrases (this great pumping up of global integration") or the biblical reference "We will reap what we sow." and clear, straightforward sentences (including shortened/elliptic and one-word sentences).
- A message which is presented through the language as necessary and urgent, e.g. by expressions with a clearly negative connotation e.g. "moral indifference", "a foolish betrayal"/pointing out negative consequences ("Failure will mean …") und unacceptable alternatives ("… if we leave millions of the world's poorest out of …").
- Contact between reader and audience is rhetorically established by informal expressions e.g. "Well, …" or a humorous comment/joke ("… it was certainly the most relaxed part of the week …), (first-person plural) personal pronouns (we, our, us), direct appeals ("Calculate …", "So let us act.").

© Ernst Klett Verlag GmbH, Stuttgart 2008 | www.klett.de
Von dieser Druckvorlage ist die Vervielfältigung für den eigenen Unterrichtsgebrauch gestattet. Die Kopiergebühren sind abgegolten. Alle Rechte vorbehalten.

Abi Workshop Englisch
Globalisation Lehrerheft
ISBN 978-3-12-601012-2

EH Erwartungshorizont

- Emphasis is rhetorically placed on key ideas by enumeration and anaphora, emphatic sentence beginnings (e.g. "Barely a week goes by without …", "What is obvious now …"), intensifying adverbs (e.g. seriously, urgently) and adjectives (e.g. pressing).

4 Evaluation: comment

- Comment on Blair's four global challenges with arguments, e.g. by rankings, prioritisation, additions to the list.
- Comment on Blair's point that it is in (Britain's) national interest to address global challenges and examples, e.g. the threats to national security by global terrorism and to national prosperity by restrictions in the energy supply or free trade.
- Comment on Blair's demand for joint action with e.g. examples from the text (e.g. follow-up agreements to the Kyoto protocol) or references to the role of the United Nations or the G8.
- Comment on Blair's demand for joint action from different perspectives, e.g. from his/her personal perspective (e.g. what he/she can contribute in everyday life)/from the perspective of the developed countries (e.g. contracts).
- Further references to the text or contextual knowledge, e.g. to common values like freedom, democracy, justice and their global acceptance/the work of global political/economic institutions (e.g. UN, EU, World Bank) and the contribution they can make to solving global challenges.

5 Composition/Text production

- Further information about the speaker, e.g. his political role, the reason for his invitation, his relationship to Tony Blair and Britain.
- Reference to, and comments on, selected statements from Blair's speech.
- Arguing in the role and from the perspective of the Indian speaker, e.g. by clearly representing Indian interests, considering the special relationship between India and Britain, voicing criticism politely and carefully.
- Falling back on contextual knowledge about India, e.g. what India`s top global challenges are/India's economic and political role in the world/etc.
- Observing the norms of the text format "political speech", e.g. introduction – middle part – conclusion/functional use of selected rhetorical devices/etc.

6 Translation

Kaum eine Woche vergeht, ohne dass ein weiteres Land in die Liste der Opfer/Ziele aufgenommen wird: Jordanien, Ägypten, Indonesien, Indien und natürlich hier in London. Kürzlich scheint ein Anschlag in Australien vereitelt worden zu sein. Alleine seit dem 7. Juni haben wir zwei Gruppen aufgedeckt, die Anschläge hier in Großbritannien geplant haben. Für alle ist es jetzt offensichtlich, dass dieses eine globale Bewegung ist, die als entsprechende Antwort auch globales Handeln erfordert. Der erfolgreiche Abschluss des demokratischen Prozesses in Afghanistan und im Irak ist ein zentraler Bestandteil dieser globalen Handlungsbereitschaft. Dieses gilt in gleicher Weise für den Friedensprozess zwischen Israel und Palästina.

Topic 2: Textinformation

Autor:	Deborah Zabarenko
Titel:	Going the Distance: Food Miles and Global Warming
	Published on Wednesday, October 17, 2007 by Reuters
Quelle:	www.commondreams.org/archive/2007/10/17/4632/ (geprüft: 23.07.2008)
Textformat/Textlänge:	Zeitungsartikel, 704 Wörter

Erwartungshorizont

1 Comprehension

a) It is assumed that eating local food reduces global warming. Food-miles give consumers an idea about the origin of their food. But its carbon footprint is a better indicator of the influence on the environment. Being produced closer to home does not always mean a smaller carbon footprint. In the US the local food movement is relatively young. Imported food has been something special for a long time. Food-miles measurements only applied to produce, not to prepared food. Some people make their choices because of taste, others because of the economic aspect. A restaurant owner criticises that in Iowa not many crops are produced for human consumption. People are interested in the origin of their food and taste is also important. The head of a consumer campaign asks for more food and less commodity farming.

(146 words)

b) • food miles (distance from production site to consumer)
- carbon footprint (takes into account: mode of transport, production methods, packaging, etc.)
- sometimes locally produced food has a higher carbon footprint
- some decades ago, only few people were interested in the origin of their food
- now more aspects are important, such as: taste, the economic aspect and where it comes from
- latest problem: much farmland used for commodity farming instead of production for human consumption

2 Form/Analysis

a) Means in language and style – effect:
1. personification/metaphor – creates pictures in the mind, makes text beautiful
   potato and its … cousin – winner in the local food derby – food miles – carbon footprint – US came late – high-end eateries – food deserts – regions lose ability to feed themselves
2. alliteration – agreeable sound
   energy-efficient – ear to eat – better-tasting taco … trucked
3. repetition – emphasis
   corn, corn everywhere
4. irony – humorous effect
   granola bar folks
5. rhetorical question – at the ending to make the reader think
6. choice of words – make the text more interesting, because they are unusual words
   edibles – gauge – provenance – locavores – restaurateur – provisions – eateries
7. quotations – add credibility

b) • clearly pro-local
- questions the calculation by food-miles
- favours calculation by carbon footprint
- gives two convincing examples that support calculation by carbon footprint: Idaho vs. Maine potato, Swedish vs. Spanish tomato
- another argument to support her view: even before eating locally became fashionable people ate locally out of necessity
- more arguments for local food: taste, economy
- she points to development
- ends with rhetorical question that should make the reader think about it

3 Discussion/Comment

a) Students might refer to the facts from the text or others e.g. from the textbook.

Food miles
- Distance food is transported from production site to consumer.
- People like food grown or produced far away or out-of-season (strawberries in winter, nuts from Australia, steak from South America).
- Don't take into account how they are produced.
- Transport is only one aspect that influences the environment.
- However, air-freight is a growing industry, so emissions will rise.

Carbon footprint
- Represents the emissions caused in the production and in transportation.
- If food is produced organically e.g. in Africa, its carbon footprint might be smaller than conventionally produced food in Europe.
- Takes into consideration the energy used in food processing, which might be lower than the amount of energy used in Europe (climate, sunshine duration).
- Students might remember this quote from E. Wagenhöfer: "You should think about where your food comes from and how it is produced …".

EH Erwartungshorizont

- Best solution: buy locally and organically produced or seasonable food.
- But this is unrealistic (choice of food, expensive).
- Fast-food generation, convenience food.
- Depend on their parents' decisions (time available, income).

b) Students will represent various attitudes. Here are some aspects they might mention:

Americans	Germans
• local food movement has become mainstream (used to be elite, expensive) • influence of environmentalists • food safety, health, taste are important • economic aspect of farming	• same: was for people with alternative lifestyles • now: lots of "Bioläden/Supermärkte, renaissance of local farmer's markets • being green has become fashionable • very health-conscious • same • probably just patriotic (potatoes, apples from the neighbourhood instead of imported produce) • but: price-conscious (low-cost imports because parents don't have so much money to spend) • depending on the area you live (people in the countryside have other options and habits than those living in city areas) • attitude: anti-globalisation • availability

c)
- Students might ask some questions.
- Show some conflicts and contradictions.
- Point out the difficulty of solving this dilemma.
- Different answers for consumers/local farmers/farmers in developing countries/supermarkets (which have to provide organic food).
- Is it okay to air-freight food?
- Can it still be called organic then?
- Should flown-in food be banned?
- What should take the priority (environment or producers of food)?
- Organic vs. FairTrade.
- Local vs. import.
- Local vs. non-organic/conventional.
- Local/small-scale farmer vs. industrial-size farming.
- Can the organic/local movement encourage sustainable agriculture? Political question?

Topic 3: Textinformation

Autor: Unknown
Titel: Queen opens new $8.6B airport terminal
Published on Friday, March 14, 2008 by CNN
Quelle: http://edition.cnn.com/2008/WORLD/europe/03/14/queen.heathrow/index.html
(geprüft: 23.07.2008)
Textformat/Textlänge: Nachrichtenartikel, 422 Wörter

Erwartungshorizont

1 Comprehension

a) Queen opens new costly terminal at Heathrow. It is owned by BAA. The passenger numbers are expected to double. There are protests by residents and environmentalists but the company wants to expand further. Greenpeace and FoE criticise the plans as environmentally irresponsible and unnecessary. Business groups and tourism executives are in favour of the expansion and consider it economically valuable.   *(60 words)*

b)

For	Against
• vital to help Britain stay competitive • domestic flights provide boost • makes it more pleasant for tourists • improves services for tourists, improves reputation	• monument to binge-flying • more flights mean more emissions, more climate change • must be the last new terminal • environmentally irresponsible, unnecessary

2 Form/Analysis

a) Author has subdivided his text in three parts of similar length:
part 1: facts (ll. 1–23),
part 2: arguments against the new terminal (ll. 24–34),
part 3: arguments for it (ll. 35–52).
This structure makes the text objective as the reader can read the facts and then compare the four negative aspects with the four positive aspects and afterwards form his/her own opinion. However, the texts ends with a positive (i.e. for the terminal) argument which could make a lasting impression on the reader.
- Quotes come from experts.
- No attitudinal adverbs.
- Neutral to formal style.

Conclusion: the author succeeds in making this text objective.

b) • Heathrow has the most passengers.
- Biggest volume of freight (1,310,987 metric tonnes).
- Followed by Gatwick as for passenger numbers and
- Stanstead which comes third as for number of passengers but second as for cargo.
- Edinburgh has the lowest number of international passengers but a relatively high number of domestic passengers compared to Birmingham or Bristol.

The following facts are supported by the data from the table:
- Heathrow is one of the world's most important transport hubs.
- Leader in domestic flights.
- Has most aircraft movements; consequently big polluter (more emissions).
- It isn't necessary for the economy of London to expand because there are already four London airports.
- The numbers (esp. airplane movements, freight in tonnes) show that aviation is a thriving economy.

c) • formal choice of words (launch, l. 2; rejuvenation, l. 3; vociferous, l. 15; alleviate, l. 47)
- numbers, data ($8.6 B; 1955, l. 6; 15 years, l. 10; 122 million a year, l. 14)
- metaphorical expression (in the pipeline, l. 15; monument to the binge-flying culture, ll. 24/25; state-of-the-art baggage management, ll. 49/50)
- passive constructions (was arrested, l. 8; were told, l. 20)
- numerous quotations
- parallelism (more flights, more emissions and more climate change, ll. 28/29)
- alliteration (protracted planning process)

3 Discussion/Comment

a) Number of low-cost airlines, and passengers who use them, rise.

	Pros	Cons
for passengers	• cheap (if booked in advance) • easy to book via the internet • fast means of transport, esp. long distances	• no service ("no frills") • doubtful booking safety • must be booked well in advance, no refund if one can't fly • crowded terminals • tax on fuel ever-increasing

© Ernst Klett Verlag GmbH, Stuttgart 2008 | www.klett.de
Von dieser Druckvorlage ist die Vervielfältigung für den eigenen Unterrichtsgebrauch gestattet. Die Kopiergebühren sind abgeolten. Alle Rechte vorbehalten.

Abi Workshop Englisch
Globalisation Lehrerheft
ISBN 978-3-12-601012-2

EH Erwartungshorizont

for the environment		• biggest polluter • people use them for short trips (weekend trips, shopping in New York, for example) • lots of noise in airport vicinity
for the economy	• provides employment for many people	• huge competition • price/wage dumping • security might suffer

b)
- Heathrow is already the busiest airport.
- More tourists can come and probably will, because a new terminal is attractive (less waiting, smoother check-in procedure, better baggage management).
- Agree with J. Bidwell that pressure on passenger will be reduced.
- Improve reputation of the airport as busy but efficient and thus attract more tourists.
- Could work as a kind of advertisement.
- Will make London as a tourist destination more appealing for people who hate waiting at airports and have refrained from going there before.

c)
- The UK has many big airports, the busiest are in the London area.
- Not only passengers but also freight (students will provide numbers from the table).
- New terminal was very expensive ($8.6B).
- Took 15 years of planning.
- Expected to double passenger numbers.
- Owned by BAA (Spanish).
- Lots of protests because bad for environment, furthers climate change (students might refer to knowledge from the SPURT text and related research).
- Students will probably be critical of the development.

Topic 4: Textinformation

Autor: Ban Ki-moon
Titel: Address to the International Conference on Terrorism: Dimensions, Threats and Counter-Measures, 15 November 2007
Quelle: www.un.org/apps/news/infocus/sgspeeches/search_full.asp?statID=149 (geprüft: 23.07.2008)
Textformat/Textlänge: Sachtext (politische Rede), 783 Wörter

Erwartungshorizont

1 Comprehension

- Historical context: the events of 9/11 – war on terrorism – interventions in Afghanistan/Iraq – limited success – Global Counter-Terrorism Strategy adopted by the UN in September 2006
- Topics: the Global Counter-Terrorism Strategy – conditions conducive to the spread of terrorism – experiences and best practices – ...
- Aims: to improve international cooperation in the struggle against terrorism – to advance the implementation of the Counter-Terrorism Strategy – ...
- Role of the UN: to provide assistance – to set standards – to provide a platform for sharing lessons and ideas – to be a partner in analysing initiatives – to give advice – ...

2 Mediation

- *Kontext der Konferenz: der Terrorismus als globale Bedrohung seit dem 11.09.2001 – die Notwendigkeit internationaler Zusammenarbeit*

- *Themen: die Globale Anti-Terrorismus Strategie der Vereinten Nationen aus dem Jahre 2006 – begünstigende Faktoren für Terrorismus – Erfahrungen mit der o.g. Strategie – erfolgreiche Konzepte – …*
- *Ziele: die Verbesserung der internationalen Kooperation – die Implementierung der o.g. Strategie weiterzuführen – …*
- *Die UN (repräsentiert durch ihren Generalsekretär): bietet Unterstützung und Rat an – legt Standards fest – bietet eine Plattform für den Austausch von Erfahrungen und Ideen – hilft bei der Analyse von Initiativen – …*

3 Analysis

- Clear text structure – sections e.g.: polite beginning (thank you to the hosts) – looking back to the Global Counter-Terrorism Strategy – aims of the conference – conditions conducive to terrorism – international cooperation – the role of the UN – conclusion with hopes for the conference
- The tone of the speaker is respectful/sober but also hopeful/confident and thus reflects his serious message to the representatives from the UN Member States.
- The content of the speech corresponds to the tone/message in the speaker's emphasis on the threat of terrorism, the need for continuing international collaboration/cooperation and the constructive role of the United Nations.
- The language fits the occasion and the message: formal English with varied but clear sentence structures and an extended register of diplomatic and political phrases.
- The language is marked by rhetorical devices which aim to
  - emphasise statements (e.g. by anaphora, enumeration, the repetition of key words, comparatives),
  - win the support of the audience (e.g. the pronoun "we", the phrase "let me …"),
  - illustrate ideas (e.g. by common metaphors like "milestone", "path").

4 Evaluation: comment

- References to the Ban Ki-moon speech.
- References to the current political situation in the world – trouble spots, conflict regions.
- Examples of conditions conducive to terrorism (cf. ll. 41–47), comparison of factors.
- Assessment of the chances of international cooperation in combating terrorism with references to various global players like the United States and other nation states, the UN or the EU.

5 Composition/Text production

- Suitable headline – first paragraph answering the wh-questions who/where/when/why: time and place, participants, topics and aims of the conference.
- Reference to, and comments on, selected statements from the Ban Ki-moon speech.
- Falling back on contextual knowledge about terrorism.
- Assessment of the relevance of the conference in the global war on terrorism.

6 Translation

Terroristen können (zum einen) Schwachstellen und Kritikpunkte ausnutzen, um Extremismus auf lokaler Ebene zu erzeugen, aber sie können (in gleicher Weise) sich auch mit anderen Terroristen international vernetzen. In gleicher Weise/Entsprechend erfordert der Kampf gegen den Terrorismus von uns den globalen Austausch von Erfahrungen und erfolgreichen Aktionen/Strategien. Und indem wir zusammen unser Augenmerk den Bedingungen zuwenden, die die Ausbreitung des Terrorismus befördern, können wir die internationale Zusammenarbeit in Sicherheits- und Rechtsfragen sinnvoll ergänzen. Lassen Sie mich eines deutlich sagen: Wenn wir uns für die Menschenrechte einsetzen, Armut und Marginalisierung bekämpfen, wenn wir versuchen, Konflikte zu lösen, gute Regierungsformen zu unterstützen und dem Recht Geltung zu verschaffen, so tun wir dieses, weil diese Aktivitäten einen Wert für sich selbst darstellen und um ihrer selbst willen verfolgt werden sollten.

RF | Revision files

Erwartungshorizont zu den *Revision files*

Revision file 1: Global challenges (Topic 1)

Since World War II

Globalisation ('global village')

Technological progress in science/technology and political stability

- multinational companies going global for markets and labour
- breakthroughs in hardware, including telephones, PCs ...
- steady flow of money and goods between international markets and production sites
- increasing mobility of people (business travellers, tourists, immigrants or refugees)
- microelectronics revolution (computers, mobile phones, etc.)
- invention of the World Wide Web/the Internet
- progress in genetic engineering, nanotechnology, computerised production methods
- efficient transportation methods
- peace in the western world after World War II
- the foundation of global political/economic institutions (NATO/the European Union/the World Bank/the IMF)
- the founding of the United Nations (peacekeeping strategies)
- détente /the breakdown of communism
- open borders/easy migration

Economic globalisation

- activities of global players
- priorities: efficiency, speed, flexibility and profit
- steady flow of money and goods (global markets and trade)
- international production chains/sites (global production)
- multinational companies produce wherever labour and overhead costs are cheapest (global players)
- global collaboration and competition

Technological globalisation

- rapid advances in technology: micro-electronics revolution
- better communication, more efficient
- rapid distribution of information
- easy, fast and efficient ways of communication
- technological co-operation

Cultural globalisation

- spread of previously local or national cultural phenomena around the world, e.g. sports, the arts, fashion, food, religion, and music
- global spread (and clash) of ideas and values
- sports (e.g. the US National Basketball League)
- fashion, religion and music
- tourism and travelling
- fast food chains operating worldwide

Revision file 2: Globalisation – different perspectives (Topic 1)

	Advantages/hopes	Criticism/fears
Industrial world	• increased business opportunities • access to new markets • affordable and reliable energy supply • fewer wars and conflicts worldwide • tourism and traveling • spread of democracy • greater understanding, and western values • cultural exchanges • peaceful, borderless world of shared values, economic prosperity and ecological stability	• difficulty in controlling power of multinational companies by legal means • inequality, regional and ethnic tensions • pollution • erosion of national cultures • massive illegal immigration • clash of cultures • rise of fundamentalism • loss of jobs and decreasing incomes at home • fierce competition in a global market • exploitation of workers in developing countries ('sweatshops')
Developing countries	• spread of freedom, democracy and human rights • greater understanding among peoples around the world • work and prosperity • participation in global trade • new markets for native products • investments in infrastructure (roads, schools, etc.) • end of hunger and ill health	• more corrupt governments, negative cultural influences and manipulation through the mass media • inequality and regional and ethnic tensions • pollution • inhumane, competitive world • widening of gap between rich and poor • increasing dependence on foreign support, investment and credit • erosion of local cultures by negative western influences

© Ernst Klett Verlag GmbH, Stuttgart 2008 | www.klett.de
Von dieser Druckvorlage ist die Vervielfältigung für den eigenen Unterrichtsgebrauch gestattet. Die Kopiergebühren sind abgegolten. Alle Rechte vorbehalten.

Globalisation
ISBN 978-3-12-601012-2

Revision file 3: Environmental effects of globalisation (Topic 2–3)

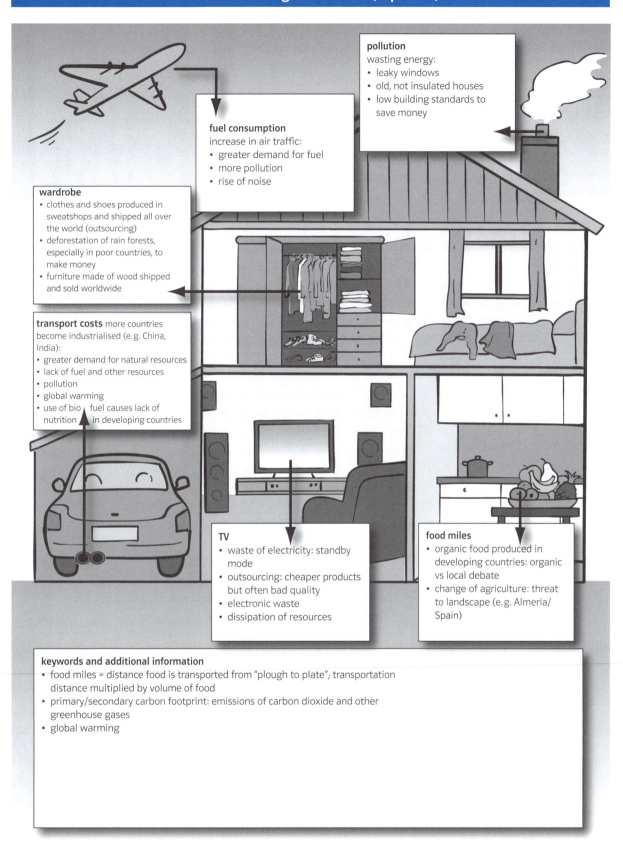

pollution wasting energy:
- leaky windows
- old, not insulated houses
- low building standards to save money

fuel consumption increase in air traffic:
- greater demand for fuel
- more pollution
- rise of noise

wardrobe
- clothes and shoes produced in sweatshops and shipped all over the world (outsourcing)
- deforestation of rain forests, especially in poor countries, to make money
- furniture made of wood shipped and sold worldwide

transport costs more countries become industrialised (e.g. China, India):
- greater demand for natural resources
- lack of fuel and other resources
- pollution
- global warming
- use of bio fuel causes lack of nutrition in developing countries

TV
- waste of electricity: standby mode
- outsourcing: cheaper products but often bad quality
- electronic waste
- dissipation of resources

food miles
- organic food produced in developing countries: organic vs local debate
- change of agriculture: threat to landscape (e.g. Almeria/Spain)

keywords and additional information
- food miles = distance food is transported from "plough to plate"; transportation distance multiplied by volume of food
- primary/secondary carbon footprint: emissions of carbon dioxide and other greenhouse gases
- global warming

RF Revision files

Revision file 4: International peacekeeping (Topic 4)

Individual countries

global political players:
- United States of America
- United Kingdom
- Russia
- France
- Germany

Supranational organisations*
- United Nations (UN)
- NATO
- African Union (AU)
- European Union (EU)
- The World Bank/International Monetary Fund (IMF)

War, terrorism and other global problems
- Arab-Israel conflict
- Darfur conflict
- Afghanistan and Iraq
- worldwide terrorism
- widening of gap between poor and rich
- climate change and other environment issues
- climate change/global warming
- access to drinking water
- sanitation and health care
- illiteracy
- poverty
- HIV/AIDS and other infectious diseases/ viruses
- fundamentalist movements
- the energy supply

Others
- influential spiritual leaders, e.g. the Pope, the Dalai Lama
- non-profit organisations (NPOs), e.g. Oxfam, Bill and Melinda Gates Foundation
- individuals like writers, activists, companies (banks, arms industry) etc.

NGOs
- Seeds of Peace
- Human Rights Watch
- Amnesty International
- Greenpeace
- Friends of the Earth
- The Red Cross
- Care
- World Vision
- Save the Children

*organisations of countries

Country/ Organisation/ Other	Structure	Aims	Methods/ Decision-making
United Nations	• General Assembly (192 nations) • Security Council (five permanent plus ten non-permanent members) • General Assembly • and other councils, agencies, etc.	• peace and security in the world • to maintain international peace and security • to develop friendly relations among nations • to cooperate in solving global problems • to promote respect for human rights	• preventive diplomacy • peacekeeping and peace-building actions • decisions based on agreement and cooperation • resolutions • peace-making operations • emergency assistance
e.g. Amnesty International	• mostly volunteers and a few paid professionals organised in ca. 50 "sections" or "structures" worldwide (represented in the) International Council	• to draw attention to human rights abuses	• decisions are made in the International Executive Committee
Seeds of Peace	• professionals and volunteers • NGO: independent of governments	• peaceful coexistence of 'enemies' in conflict areas	• provision of training and intercultural exchange
e.g. the European Union	three main institutions: – European Commission, – European Parliament, – Council of Ministers	to promote: – peace, prosperity, stability – economic and social development – shared values – a sound environment	the three main institutions negotiate and adopt: – treaties – laws – regulations – recommendations
USA	• Congress: Senate and House of Representatives (legislative branch) • President and Cabinet (executive branch)	• control of various threats • building of democratic societies	• military intervention • active diplomacy, treaties, economic pressure

© Ernst Klett Verlag GmbH, Stuttgart 2008 | www.klett.de
Von dieser Druckvorlage ist die Vervielfältigung für den eigenen Unterrichtsgebrauch gestattet. Die Kopiergebühren sind abgegolten. Alle Rechte vorbehalten.

Abi Workshop Englisch
Globalisation Lehrerheft
ISBN 978-3-12-601012-2